Faith Greater than
Our Challenges

Faith Greater than Our Challenges

What the Apostle Paul and Viktor Frankl
Can Teach Us about Difficult Times

TOM EDMONDSON

Foreword by Alexandros Pattakos

WIPF & STOCK · Eugene, Oregon

FAITH GREATER THAN OUR CHALLENGES
What the Apostle Paul and Viktor Frankl Can Teach Us about Difficult
Times

Wipf & Stock
An Imprint of Wipf and Stock Publishers
199 W. 8th Ave., Suite 3
Eugene, OR 97401

www.wipfandstock.com

PAPERBACK ISBN: 978-1-6667-3038-8
HARDCOVER ISBN: 978-1-6667-2181-2
EBOOK ISBN: 978-1-6667-2182-9

11/04/21

Ann, my companion and soul mate in all of life's circumstances. No one knows better than you how much I needed to learn the lessons related here. With love and appreciation, I dedicate this book to you!

Contents

Foreword by Alexandros Pattakos   ix

Acknowledgments   xiii

Introduction   xv

How to Approach This Book   xvii

Principle 1: Exercise the Freedom to Choose Your Attitude   1

Principle 2: Realize Your Will to Meaning   8

Principle 3: Detect the Meaning of Life's Moments   15

Principle 4: Don't Work against Yourself   21

Principle 5: Look at Yourself from a Distance   27

Principle 6: Shift Your Focus of Attention   35

Principle 7: Extend beyond Yourself   42

Principle 8: Responsibleness   49

Principle 9: Maintain Your Integrity   57

Personal Application   65

Conclusion   67

Bibliography   69

Foreword

In January 2021, Rev. Tom Edmondson, the senior pastor of the First Christian Church of Atlanta, Georgia, approached us to request permission to use the core principles in our book *Prisoners of Our Thoughts: Viktor Frankl's Principles for Discovering Meaning in Life and Work* (3rd edition) as the structure of a series of weekly sermons to help his congregation deal with—and find meaning in—the broad-based effects and implications of the coronavirus (COVID-19) pandemic. My coauthor, Elaine Dundon, and I were especially honored by this request since Rev. Edmondson proposed to integrate the principles alongside the ageless wisdom espoused by the world-renowned psychiatrist Viktor E. Frankl in his classic bestseller *Man's Search for Meaning* with lessons from the composite letter of Paul to the Philippians, also called the Epistle of St. Paul the Apostle to the Philippians.

Against the backdrop of the pandemic, political divide in America, and other formidable challenges during this difficult time, Rev. Edmondson's series of sermons, which he described as "a call of faith greater than our challenges," was especially timely and much needed. I believe that it was this *call of faith* that rightly led Rev. Edmondson to the letter of Paul to the Philippians as the origin of and impetus behind his inspirational, *meaning*-focused sermons. Moreover, by choosing to apply Dr. Frankl's system of logotherapy and existential analysis in parallel with the teachings of the apostle

Foreword

Paul, Rev. Edmondson added a unique and universal value to his message from the pastor's pulpit.

Indeed, Paul's letter to the Philippians proved to be a perfect match with and complement to Dr. Frankl's teachings and life experience. In both cases, the *call of faith greater than our challenges* could be heard loud and clear, and provided a similar base for action. In this connection, Frankl's extraordinary personal story of finding meaning amid the horrors of the Nazi concentration camps during World War II has inspired millions of people around the world. As Rev. Edmondson describes so eloquently in this insightful book, the apostle Paul's letter, which was one of his prison epistles, is equally inspiring and meaningful in its own profoundly moving way. Despite being a prisoner facing possible execution, Paul was able to discover that his faith enabled him to rise above the personal suffering he was forced to endure and, importantly, find deep meaning, including a sense of clarity, in the face of his unjust imprisonment.

The similarities between the attitudes of the apostle Paul and Viktor Frankl, especially toward inescapable suffering, imprisonment, and the impending threat of death, are both striking and instructive. Among other things, they are grounded in unwavering faith, are life-affirming, and unequivocally demonstrate that even in our most desperate situations and darkest times, we always have what Dr. Frankl called the "last of the human freedoms"—to choose our attitude in response to life circumstances. Importantly, it is this ultimate freedom, as both the apostle Paul and Dr. Frankl aptly demonstrate by their life example, that guides us along the path to deep meaning in life no matter what.

Perhaps one of the most often-quoted passages from Viktor Frankl's work is the following from his book *Man's Search for Meaning*: "You do not have to suffer to learn. But, if you don't learn from suffering, over which you have no control, then your life becomes truly meaningless. . . . The way in which a man accepts his fate—those things beyond his control—can add a deeper meaning to his life. He controls how he responds."[1] In this book, Rev. Edmondson

1. Frankl, *Man's Search for Meaning*, 117.

demonstrates in no uncertain terms how the apostle Paul and Dr. Viktor Frankl practiced what they preached by answering life's call with a faith greater than their challenges. As a result, they both embraced life with meaning and left legacies filled with ageless wisdom that will forever bring light to darkness.

ALEX PATTAKOS, PHD
Coauthor of *Prisoners of Our Thoughts: Viktor Frankl's Principles for Discovering Meaning in Life and Work* (3rd edition)

Acknowledgments

This book also exists because of the following wonderful congregations: First Christian Church of Atlanta (Disciples of Christ) in Tucker, GA and First Christian Church of Griffin (Disciples of Christ) in Griffin, GA.

Special Thanks

A special word of thanks goes to Alexandros (Alex) Pattakos and Elaine Dundon, authors of *Prisoners of Our Thoughts: Viktor Frankl's Principles for Discovering Meaning in Life and Work* (3rd edition). Your wonderful book makes the vast work of Viktor Frankl accessible and relatable to nonspecialists. Not only does it help people find meaning in life by applying Dr. Frankl's work on logotherapy and existential analysis to their lives, but it also gave me a perfect framework for relating Paul's letter to the Philippians to Dr. Frankl's work. Alex and Elaine, you have been generous and supportive throughout this process. I am grateful for your friendship!

Thanks to Ann Edmondson, Nate Martin, and Johnathan and Eden Clark for reading the manuscript for this book and providing valuable insights toward its improvement! It is a better book thanks to you!

Introduction

This book seeks to demonstrate a positive way to deal with any set of circumstances, no matter how difficult. Originally, each chapter was a message I delivered as senior pastor of First Christian Church of Atlanta (Disciples of Christ) from January 24 through March 21, 2021 during the COVID-19 pandemic. My goal as the months of quarantine dragged on was to deliver messages that encouraged my congregation to be patient and find meaning in the isolation, boredom, and loss.

As I sought a direction, Viktor Frankl's bestseller, *Man's Search for Meaning*, kept emerging in my thoughts as a good place to start. Here was a book about someone who had experienced loss and isolation on a horrific scale during the Shoah (Holocaust). After losing his wife and his parents in the camps, he survived three years of Nazi brutality in four different camps, including Auschwitz. Through it all, and for many decades after, Frankl affirmed that even in those circumstances, life has meaning, and it is the responsibility of each person to find that meaning.

But how to present Frankl's work in the form of a sermon series was a conundrum. While *Man's Search for Meaning* is very accessible, it only introduces logotherapy and existential analysis. A fuller presentation of his thought meant drawing from his wider work, which is more academic and challenging. Is this something a pastor has time to read, digest, and reproduce on a week-to-week basis?

Introduction

Thankfully, this problem only occupied me for a short time because I realized that this task had already been done for me. Alexandros (Alex) Pattakos and Elaine Dundon, authors of *Prisoners of Our Thoughts: Viktor Frankl's Principles for Discovering Meaning in Life and Work* (3rd edition), had taken the body of Viktor Frankl's work and distilled it into seven easy-to-understand principles. So, the task for me became to find passages of Scripture that accurately matched up with these principles.

And then I realized that Paul's letter to the Philippians is the perfect complement to *Man's Search for Meaning*. In this letter, we learn that Paul was in prison and facing possible execution. Yet he expressed a sense of meaning and even joy in his circumstances, which he also commended to the recipients of that letter. And as I began to read through Philippians with Alex and Elaine's framework for explaining Viktor Frankl's body of work, the job became easier and quite pleasurable. Everything came together beautifully. From these three sources we discover that faith in God, in life, and in ourselves can elevate us above any circumstance and give a sense of purpose and meaning, strength, and joy.

I believe the lessons in this book are timeless, but they were written and delivered at a very dramatic time. The COVID-19 pandemic being of worldwide scope affected the lives of practically every living person on earth. At the same time, the United States was going through the tumultuous and contested 2020 US presidential election season and much racial tension. Add to this people's individual experiences of isolation and loss and you have conditions conducive to depression and hopelessness.

As a minister speaking to a variety of people, all affected by these circumstances, I felt the call to speak truth and hope that would help them see beyond the present moment. So as you read, keep in mind that these messages make references to what we were in the midst of experiencing in January through March of 2021. But in no way does this detract from the timelessness of the messages—rather, it gives them relevance.

How to Approach This Book

Logotherapy and *existential analysis* are two terms that describe Viktor Frankl's approach to psychotherapy. Thus, this book is a *logotherapeutic* reading of Paul's letter to the Philippians. This means that I will be drawing comparisons between what Paul wrote theologically about suffering during his imprisonment and what Viktor Frankl taught psychologically about his suffering and experiences in the camps.

This book is not in any way a baptism—or Christianization—of Viktor Frankl or logotherapy. Its goal is to demonstrate the similarities between Paul's and Viktor Frankl's attitudes toward imprisonment, the threat of death, and what they can teach us about a life-affirming attitude in our own darkest challenges. Notably, it is not the first logotherapeutic reading of a religious text, as there are many fine Jewish and Christian readings that have preceded this one.

Neither Paul's letter to the Philippians nor Frankl's work is treated here in chronological order. It is arranged topically based on the seven principles of Viktor Frankl's teaching as formulated by Alex Pattakos and Elaine Dundon in *Prisoners of Our Thoughts*. I have added two more principles for a total of nine. These nine principles make up the body of this book. Each principle is illustrated with passages from Philippians and the work of Dr. Frankl.

How to Approach This Book

The nine principles of Dr. Frankl's work that make up the chapters of this book are as follows:

1. Exercise the freedom to choose your attitude.
2. Realize your will to meaning.
3. Detect the meaning of life's moments.
4. Don't work against yourself.
5. Look at yourself from a distance.
6. Shift your focus of attention.
7. Extend beyond yourself.[2]
8. Responsibleness.
9. Maintain Your Integrity.

2. The first seven principles are taken directly from Pattakos and Dundon, *Prisoners of Our Thoughts*, 4–7.

Principle 1

Exercise the Freedom to Choose Your Attitude

Scripture selection: Phil 1:15–26

Some proclaim Christ from envy and rivalry, but others from goodwill. These proclaim Christ out of love, knowing that I have been put here for the defense of the gospel; the others proclaim Christ out of selfish ambition, not sincerely but intending to increase my suffering in my imprisonment. What does it matter? Just this, that Christ is proclaimed in every way, whether out of false motives or true; and in that I rejoice. Yes, and I will continue to rejoice, for I know that through your prayers and the help of the Spirit of Jesus Christ this will turn out for my deliverance. It is my eager expectation and hope that I will not be put to shame in any way, but that by my speaking with all boldness, Christ will be exalted now as always in my body, whether by life or by death. For to me, living is Christ and dying is gain. If I am to live in the flesh, that means fruitful labor for me; and I do not know which I prefer. I am hard pressed between the two: my desire is to depart and be with Christ, for that is far better; but to remain in the flesh is more necessary for you. Since I am convinced of this, I know that I will remain and continue with all of you for your progress and joy in

faith, so that I may share abundantly in your boasting in
Christ Jesus when I come to you again.

January 24, 2021

This is the first of nine messages that draw from Paul's Letter to the
Philippians and the psychology of Viktor Frankl. I chose Paul's letter to the Philippians because he wrote it from prison. In it he states
that he did not know whether he would be released or executed.
He also wrote about opponents and critics who were adding to his
burden. But while facing opposition and certain death, Paul penned
this hopeful little letter to encourage the Philippian congregation
to keep the faith. Paul's steadfast courage and sense of conviction
despite his circumstances have been inspiring to many Christians
throughout the last twenty centuries.

I chose Viktor Frankl for similar reasons. Dr. Frankl was a neu-
rologist and physician in Vienna, Austria who, along with his wife
and parents, was sent to a concentration camp in 1942 by the Nazis.
In three years' time, Frankl lost everything: his wife and parents all
perished. Despite these painful losses and the inhuman conditions
of the camps, Frankl survived. His book *Man's Search for Meaning*
recounts his experiences of loss and his survival. In it he maintains
that life has meaning, and that if we can find that meaning, we can
endure almost anything. Dr. Frankl's books and lectures have been
a source of strength for many people for over seventy years. Like the
apostle Paul, Viktor Frankl's words have been a source of hope and
inspiration for millions.

A third resource for these messages is the book *Prisoners of
Our Thoughts: Viktor Frankl's Principles for Discovering Meaning in
Life and Work* (3rd edition) by Alex Pattakos and Elaine Dundon.
In this book, Alex and Elaine have taken the scope of Frankl's work
and distilled it into seven easy-to-understand principles. When
I wrestled with how to share Paul's letter to the Philippians and
Frankl's inspiring work in these messages, I realized that these sev-
en principles provided the perfect framework for doing so. And in
my preparation, I realized there are two additional principles where

Exercise the Freedom to Choose Your Attitude

Frankl and Paul's letter to the Philippians line up nicely. So again, there will be nine messages total.

To begin, the challenges we currently face are numerous and cannot simply be summarized with words like "pandemic" and "politics." We are connected electronically but physically separated. Some people are financially secure; others are facing eviction. COVID-19 vaccines are rolling out—but not fast enough—and a more contagious strain has emerged. There are some who by all appearances are doing fine, but underneath the surface there is anxiety. Anxiety can turn into depression. The scary thing is, it can hit us before we realize it.

I am not equating our experience of isolation and loss due to COVID-19 with Viktor Frankl's experience of the Nazi concentration camps or Paul's prison experience. But in *Man's Search for Meaning*, Frankl wrote:

> A man's suffering is similar to the behavior of a gas. If a certain quantity of gas is pumped into an empty chamber, it will fill the chamber completely and evenly, no matter how big the chamber. Thus suffering completely fills the human soul and conscious mind, no matter whether the suffering is great or little. Therefore the "size" of human suffering is absolutely relative.[1]

Frankl was not one to say, "You think you have it bad! I had it worse!" He recognized, as we should, that our own experiences—no matter how they compare to his—can be all-consuming to us. For anyone who is feeling the strain of economics, isolation, sickness, political turmoil, or loss, the first principle of Frankl's teaching is essential: "Exercise the freedom to choose your attitude."

Two of the most quoted passages from *Man's Search for Meaning* read as follows: "When we are no longer able to change a situation—just think of an incurable disease such as inoperable cancer—we are challenged to change ourselves"[2] and "Everything can be taken from a man but one thing: the last of the human freedoms—to choose one's attitude in any given set of circumstances,

1. Frankl, *Man's Search for Meaning*, 43.
2. Frankl, *Man's Search for Meaning*, 112.

to choose one's *own way*."[3] These two statements are not glib clichés. Remember what he had experienced before he ever wrote these lines. If anyone had reason to give up in despair, it was Frankl. But he held to his conviction that life is meaningful. If a person has a sense of meaning, they can face anything.

Many centuries before Frankl wrote these words, Paul was in prison for preaching the gospel, was being criticized by fellow believers, and was facing possible execution. Who among us, under such circumstances, would not feel justified in throwing a pity party, or even giving up hope and succumbing to despair? And yet this letter is filled with words of thanks, gratitude, and joy. Paul, like Frankl, was able to find meaning in the most difficult of circumstances. Though separated from the Philippian congregation by distance and imprisonment, Paul modeled for them—and us—how to choose one's attitude.

In Phil 1:15–18, Paul describes some who preach the gospel with the wrong motives and others with right motives. In some way or other, the ones with wrong motives preach out of "selfish ambition" and to increase Paul's "suffering" (1:17). If this seems a little hard to understand, just imagine a room full of preachers. We are all supposed to be on the same team, but where there are theological and stylistic differences, there can often be friction, if not outright conflict. In response to this, Paul writes: "What does it matter? Just this, that Christ is proclaimed in every way, whether out of false motives or true; and in that I rejoice" (1:18).

In verses 19–26, Paul rather blithely describes his uncertainty as to whether he will survive prison to continue his ministry or be put to death. Clearly, he does not fear death, but he also feels like there is still work for him, so he writes, "I am hard pressed between the two: my desire is to depart and be with Christ, for that is far better; but to remain in the flesh is more necessary for you" (1:23–24). Though Paul writes as if uncertain about his future, what he does not do is sound despairing or hopeless. He chooses a win-win approach in that he can write "living is Christ, dying is gain" in verse 21. He can see the good in both outcomes.

3. Frankl, *Man's Search for Meaning*, 65.

Exercise the Freedom to Choose Your Attitude

Most of us are not that saintly. We probably go through a cycle of negative emotions before we can get to the more positive outlook. So be it. When you find yourself in negative mode—or hopeless mode—remember the apostle Paul in prison, or Viktor Frankl in a concentration camp, or perhaps this story related by Pattakos and Dundon in *Prisoners of Our Thoughts*:

> There is an inspiring story about Nelson Mandela. . . . At a young age, Mandela fought to change South Africa's economically and politically oppressive apartheid system and to foster racial equality. In 1962 he was arrested, convicted of conspiracy to overthrow the state, and sentenced to life imprisonment. As a result of mounting pressure from the people of South Africa and international agencies, Mandela was released from prison in 1990 after serving twenty-seven years.
>
> The day Mandela was released from prison, Bill Clinton, then governor of Arkansas, was watching the news. Clinton called to his wife and daughter: "You must see this; it is historic." As Mandela stepped out from the prison walls to be greeted by the international press, Clinton saw a flush of anger on Mandela's face as he looked at the people watching. But then the anger disappeared. Later, when Clinton was president of the United States and Mandela was president of South Africa, the two leaders met, and Clinton relayed this observation. Clinton candidly asked Mandela to explain what seemed to have occurred on that day. Mandela replied: "Yes, you are right. When I was in prison, the son of a guard started a Bible study and I attended . . . and that day when I stepped out of prison and looked at the people observing, a flush of anger hit me with the thought that they had robbed me of twenty-seven years. Then the Spirit of Jesus said to me, 'Nelson, while you were in prison you were free; now that you are free, don't become their prisoner.'" Indeed, upon his release Mandela displayed his ability, once again, to be a model for reconciliation, with no spirit of revenge or negativism. He understood

that the freedom to choose one's attitude is one of the most basic and important freedoms human beings have.[4]

What if Mandela had chosen differently? How would South Africa's history have unfolded? Or if Viktor Frankl had chosen a defeatist attitude and given up? How many countless millions of lives would not have been blessed and strengthened by his example? As it is, he outlived his captivity by about fifty-two years. He died in 1997. Finally, what if the apostle Paul had seen his captivity as the end and given up hope and faith in Jesus? Aren't we better because Paul chose an attitude of hope and faith?

How important is the attitude we choose? In many ways, attitude is everything. It is important on a personal level because it affects our peace of mind (mental health). Our ability to cope with difficult circumstances often comes down to how we think about them. It is also important on an interpersonal level because it influences our family members, our friends, and our acquaintances. How would you like to be remembered? As I wrote in the December 2020 issue of *Our Town DeKalb*:

> While our current circumstances are less than ideal, we don't have to think of them as all gloom. Imagine a time, twenty years from now, when a child asks, "What were the holidays like during the COVID-19 pandemic? How did you make it?" What would you like your answer to be? Perhaps your answer would be something like this: "I learned how to be resilient. No matter what happens in life, there is meaning to be found." And perhaps that child will hear the hope in your voice and learn from your example.[5]

4 Pattakos and Dundon, *Prisoners of Our Thoughts*, 27.

5. Edmondson, "Home for Christmas," 12.

Exercise the Freedom to Choose Your Attitude

Principle 1 Group Discussion

Pick one of the following people or groups of people from the Bible. Discuss how their experiences mirror those of the apostle Paul and Viktor Frankl:

- Joseph sold into slavery and falsely accused (Gen 37–41).
- Naomi and Ruth (Ruth 1–4).
- David persecuted by Saul (1 Sam 19–26).
- Daniel, Shadrach, Meshach, Abednego (Dan 1–6).
- Stephen (Acts 6–7).

How did the person or group exercise the freedom to choose their own attitude(s)?

Can you think of other figures in history or members of your own family who demonstrate this principle?

How can knowing these examples help you during difficult times?

Principle 2

Realize Your Will to Meaning

Scripture selection: Phil 3:4–16

If anyone else has reason to be confident in the flesh, I have more: circumcised on the eighth day, a member of the people of Israel, of the tribe of Benjamin, a Hebrew born of Hebrews; as to the law, a Pharisee; as to zeal, a persecutor of the church; as to righteousness under the law, blameless. Yet whatever gains I had, these I have come to regard as loss because of Christ. More than that, I regard everything as loss because of the surpassing value of knowing Christ Jesus my Lord. For his sake I have suffered the loss of all things, and I regard them as rubbish, in order that I may gain Christ and be found in him, not having a righteousness of my own that comes from the law, but one that comes through faith in Christ, the righteousness from God based on faith. I want to know Christ and the power of his resurrection and the sharing of his sufferings by becoming like him in his death, if somehow I may attain the resurrection from the dead.

Realize Your Will to Meaning

January 31, 2021

Can anyone tell me where the following lines are found in the Bible: "It is a far, far better thing that I do, than I have ever done; it is a far, far better rest that I go to than I have ever known"?[1] It is a trick question, of course. They come from Sydney Carton, just before dying by guillotine at the end of Charles Dickens's *A Tale of Two Cities*. They do sound biblical, don't they?

A Tale of Two Cities is set in England and France before and during the French Revolution. It has an intricate plot, colorful characters, and dramatic events. Sydney Carton is the character who changes the most out of all the characters because he goes from being a lazy alcoholic who cares for no one—not even himself—to a man who sacrifices his life in place of Charles Darnay. Why does he do this? Perhaps the answer is that by giving his life in place of another, he finally found a meaning for his life.

I think we love these kinds of sacrificial stories in literature because we find such characters sympathetic and praiseworthy. But the process of transformation seems deceptively simple; it is presented in about three hundred pages, which takes about eight hours to read. The story, however, takes place over a span of seventeen years. Similarly, when we pick up a book like *Man's Search for Meaning*—which takes less than five hours to read—we probably cannot get a real sense of the inhuman conditions Viktor Frankl experienced for three years. In other words, real life can only be experienced by you. You can describe it for us, and we can sympathize with you. We may even learn from your experience, but it is yours alone. Only you know the extent to which you worked, sacrificed, and suffered. How could anyone put all that into words?

Did you know that at least three years elapsed between the apostle Paul's Damascus Road experience[2] and his first missionary

---

1. Dickens, *Tale of Two Cities*, 335.

2. See Acts 9:1–9 for the Damascus Road experience and Acts 13 and 14 for Paul's first missionary journey. I use the term "Damascus Road experience" where others may say "conversion." I am inclined to agree with Krister Stendhal's argument in *Paul among Jews* that what happened on the road to Damascus is more properly called a "calling" than a "conversion." For the sake

journey? This short estimate is arrived at by piecing the evidence together. It could have been considerably longer. What I am interested in here is that transformation takes time. Just as Jacob's name was changed to Israel (Gen 35:10) to mark a decisive turning point in the patriarch's life, Paul's transformation was dramatic enough to warrant a name change from Saul to Paul.

When we read the words of our text today, despite Paul's positive tone, there are indications of difficulty. Notice the second half of Phil 3:8: "For his sake I have *suffered the loss of all things*, and I regard them as rubbish, in order that I may gain Christ" (emphasis mine). If we are not careful, we might completely miss the pain or difficulty that it implies. How many of us have "suffered the loss of all things"?

Might this new sensitivity to Paul's words help us to understand verse 10: "I want to know Christ and the power of his resurrection and the sharing of his sufferings by becoming like him in his death" (Phil 3:10)? Does it sound a little different now? Surely first-century Christians in the Roman Empire would know that Jesus died by crucifixion. Who in their right mind would look forward to repeating that?

Remember, Paul wrote this letter while in prison, facing possible execution, and suffering criticism from opponents who did not wish him well. Despite these facts, Paul's tone in this letter to the Philippian congregation is positive and encouraging. Why? And why is he willing to endure these hardships? The answer is that he realized his *will to meaning* in this suffering. First, by suffering for preaching the gospel, Paul was following in the footsteps of Jesus. Second, his fellow believers were emboldened by his example and unbelievers took notice. As he wrote in 1:12–14:

> What has happened to me has actually helped to spread the gospel, so that it has become known throughout the whole imperial guard and to everyone else that my imprisonment is for Christ; and most of the brothers and sisters, having been made confident in the Lord by my imprisonment, dare to speak the word with greater boldness and without fear.

---

of our study, it will suffice to refer to it as his "Damascus Road experience."

And third, as mentioned in Phil 3:10–11, Paul believed that just as Jesus was vindicated by his resurrection, believers will also be vindicated by resurrection.

Viktor Frankl identified three main avenues by which one arrives at meaning in life. The first one is "by creating a work or by doing a deed."[3] We see this illustrated by Sydney Carton in *A Tale of Two Cities* and by Frankl in *Man's Search for Meaning*. For Carton, giving his life in exchange for Darnay's was a deed that gave his life meaning. For Frankl, it was creating a work—or rather, surviving so he could rewrite his book and get it published—that gave him meaning.

Frankl's second avenue for arriving at meaning is "experiencing something or encountering someone; in other words, meaning can be found not only in work but also in love."[4] Though Carton sacrificed his life to save Darnay, it was because of his love for Lucie. As he says to Lucie: "For you, and for any dear to you, I would do anything. I would embrace any sacrifice for you and for those dear to you. And when you see your own bright beauty springing up anew at your feet, think now and then that there is a man who would give his life, to keep a life you love beside you."[5]

As for the apostle Paul, we could say that it was both his experience on the road to Damascus and his relationship with Jesus that gave his life meaning. This is what he expresses in Phil 3:8: "More than that, I regard everything as loss because of the *surpassing value of knowing Christ Jesus my Lord*. For his sake I have suffered the loss of all things, and I regard them as rubbish, in order that I may gain Christ" (emphasis mine). Saul had been driven by a personal cause, but Paul was drawn to Christ.

Frankl's third avenue to meaning is stated as follows: "Even the helpless victim facing a fate he cannot change, may rise above himself, may grow beyond himself, and by so doing change himself."[6] For Carton, it was not just that he was able to find meaning by

---

3. Frankl, *Man's Search for Meaning*, 145.
4. Frankl, *Man's Search for Meaning*, 145.
5. Dickens, *Tale of Two Cities*, 134.
6. Frankl, *Man's Search for Meaning*, 146.

giving his life in exchange for Darnay's; it also allowed him to become a virtuous person. Thus, he was able to say, "it is a far, far better thing I do, than I have ever done."[7] For Paul, it was the belief that he could glorify Jesus either by his life or his death. As we read in last week's passage: "It is my eager expectation and hope that I will not be put to shame in any way, but that by my speaking with all boldness, Christ will be exalted now as always in my body, whether by life or by death. For to me, living is Christ and dying is gain" (Phil 1:20–21).

There are three distinct schools of psychology that originated in Vienna, Austria in the twentieth century. The first was Sigmund Freud's school of psychoanalysis. The second was Alfred Adler's school of individual psychology. And third was Viktor Frankl's school of logotherapy. I mention this because I preached a sermon based on the temptation of Jesus as found in Luke 4:1–13. I related the first temptation, "If you are the Son of God, command this stone to become a loaf of bread" (Luke 4:3), to Freud's pleasure principle because the temptation was aimed at satisfying a bodily drive: hunger. For Freud, human nature is reducible to instincts and drives in a way similar to animals. Because of this, Frankl characterized Freud's thought with the phrase "the will to pleasure."[8]

In the second temptation, the devil literally offered Jesus the world in exchange for worshiping him. I related this to Adler's individual psychology because Adler believed that people are driven to seek power and fame. Frankl characterized this as "the will to power."[9] While both schools contain some truth, like Frankl, I do not believe these two theories do full justice to humanity for the simple reason that a person can have all their drives satisfied, attain all sorts of power and fame, and still feel that life is meaningless. In contrast to these two, Frankl describes his school of logotherapy, or existential psychology, as "the will to meaning."[10] This will to meaning makes us human and makes life worthwhile.

7. Dickens, *Tale of Two Cities*, 335.

8. Frankl, *Man's Search for Meaning*, 99.

9. Frankl, *Man's Search for Meaning*, 99.

10. Frankl, *Man's Search for Meaning*, 99.

Realize Your Will to Meaning

Though Sydney Carton is only a literary figure, Dickens used him to illustrate the themes of transformation and redemption. Carton is transformed from an unmotivated, self-centered lush into a virtuous, self-sacrificial hero. This happens through his interaction with Lucie and Darnay, and ultimately, through the unselfish love he develops. When living only for himself, life has no meaning; when dying for another, it does. For Frankl, even after the deaths of his wife and parents, and despite the terrible conditions of the concentration camps, he affirmed that life always has meaning. That belief sustained him and allowed him to outlive his captivity by five decades.

The apostle Paul was transformed by his experience of the risen Jesus on the road to Damascus. This new relationship gave him a sense of meaning that motivated him to undergo a difficult and dangerous life as a missionary. In 2 Cor 11:24–27, he writes:

> Five times I have received from the Jews the forty lashes minus one. Three times I was beaten with rods. Once I received a stoning. Three times I was shipwrecked; for a night and a day I was adrift at sea; on frequent journeys, in danger from rivers, danger from bandits, danger from my own people, danger from Gentiles, danger in the city, danger in the wilderness, danger at sea, danger from false brothers and sisters; in toil and hardship, through many a sleepless night, hungry and thirsty, often without food, cold and naked.

Why did he endure all that? Perhaps we could say, in Frankl's terminology, that in it he realized his will to meaning. How else could he write "to live is Christ, to die is gain" (Phil 1:21)?

It was during three years of suffering in concentration camps that Viktor Frankl affirmed his will to meaning. It was from death row that Paul affirmed his will to meaning. Many people think more money, a better job, an end to COVID-19, a certain political party being in power, or a new relationship will give their life meaning—but the truth is quite different. What we need is to find meaning regardless of the circumstances. That is where faith comes in. Life has meaning because it is given to us by God and because of the relationships we share. Even under the most difficult of

Faith Greater than Our Challenges

circumstances—pandemic conditions, an accelerating death toll, rising unemployment, and just general anxiety—life has meaning if we are willing to affirm it. Are you ready to realize your will to meaning?

Principle 2 Group Discussion

Here are some people in John's Gospel whose lives were changed by their encounter with Jesus. Discuss how the encounter helped them realize a will to meaning.

- Andrew, Peter, Philip, and Nathanael (John 2:35–50).
- The Samaritan Woman and her community (John 4).

In your own life, how has your relationship with God and others helped you realize your will to meaning?

Can you tell of a time when this will to meaning found in your faith and/or faith community has sustained you through challenging times?

Principle 3

Detect the Meaning of Life's Moments

Scripture selection: Phil 1:12–14 and 4:11b-13

I want you to know, beloved, that what has happened to me has actually helped to spread the gospel, so that it has become known throughout the whole imperial guard and to everyone else that my imprisonment is for Christ; and most of the brothers and sisters, having been made confident in the Lord by my imprisonment, dare to speak the word with greater boldness and without fear.

For I have learned to be content with whatever I have. I know what it is to have little, and I know what it is to have plenty. In any and all circumstances I have learned the secret of being well-fed and of going hungry, of having plenty and of being in need. I can do all things through him who strengthens me.

February 7, 2021

The apostle Paul and Viktor Frankl understood the meaning of hardship and suffering. Both wrote of their experiences and beliefs to provide guidance and encouragement to their readers—Paul to the believers in the churches he started, and Frankl to his patients and reading audience. Their works are complementary: from Paul we get a *theology* of resilience, and from Frankl we get a *psychology* of resilience. Both wrote from a faith perspective.

In our discussion of the first principle—"Exercise the freedom to choose your attitude"—we talked about how we may not control our circumstances but we can control how we deal with them. (This is also called emotional intelligence). Even in the face of death, Paul's faith gave him the confidence to write that "living is Christ and dying is gain" (Phil 1:21).

The message based on principle 2—"Realize your will to meaning"—stated that life, even in the worst of circumstances, has meaning. That meaning can be found in a cause, a work of art, or in a relationship. We might ask, Was Paul willing to suffer as he did because he believed in his message or because he had a life-altering experience with the risen Christ? Probably both. This thought shows the progression from principle 1 to principle 2: finding meaning is an act of the will, a choice.

This leads us to the third principle: "Detect the meaning of life's moments." In *Man's Search for Meaning*, Frankl writes: "Live as if you were living already for the second time and as if you had acted the first time as wrongly as you are about to act now!"[1] If you find this language a little hard to follow, here is how a different translator rendered it: "Act as though you have a second chance at life, and the first time around did as badly as you possibly could have."[2] Here is my attempt at simplifying it: "Every day we get a fresh start at life." In Phil 3:13b–14, Paul expressed his version of it this way: "Forgetting what lies behind and straining forward to what lies ahead, I press on toward the goal for the prize of the heavenly call of God in Christ Jesus."

Many of us do not really understand the meaning of life's moments as they happen. Only after they have passed do we grasp their significance, and that is okay. Hindsight is 20/20 . . . On the other hand, we *should* learn from our experiences. If we keep making

1. Frankl, *Man's Search for Meaning*, 114.

2. Frankl, *Rediscovery of the Human*, 27.

the same mistakes or falling into the same dysfunctional patterns of behavior, we are not detecting the meaning of life's moments. As we get older and more experienced in life, we should develop the presence of mind to understand our circumstances in a more meaning-oriented way. In other words, from *hindsight* we should learn to develop *foresight*. I think Paul's words in our two texts today demonstrate the mature faith perspective of a person who had learned to detect the meaning of life's moments.

The first text, Phil 1:12–14, is a carryover from last week's message:

> I want you to know, beloved, that what has happened to me has actually helped to spread the gospel, so that it has become known throughout the whole imperial guard and to everyone else that my imprisonment is for Christ; and most of the brothers and sisters, having been made confident in the Lord by my imprisonment, dare to speak the word with greater boldness and without fear.

In this passage, we can see how principles 1, 2, and 3 overlap. Paul basically arrived at a mature attitude toward his imprisonment and critics in that he 1) chose an attitude of rejoicing that despite opposition, Christ was being preached; 2) he realized his will to meaning in that even his suffering advanced the gospel; and 3) he detected the meaning of that moment as an opportunity to encourage the Philippian congregation to persist despite their own struggles.

In this message, I want to focus on our second text, Phil 4:11–13. Notice how it ends with one of the most famous verses in the whole letter: "I can do all things through him who strengthens me" (4:13). One of the difficult issues in interpreting this letter is figuring out when and where Paul wrote it. No one really knows. Other than the fact that he was in prison and facing execution, he does not indicate where he is. We are not going to worry about it; suffice it to say that the book of Acts ends with Paul in Rome under house arrest and church tradition tells us that Paul was executed in Rome. So, it is as good a guess as any to think he was writing in Rome near the end of his life. Whatever the case may be, both passages show us a Paul who could be magnanimous under the most trying of conditions. Was he always like that, or is it something he learned?

Among other things, the letter to the Philippians is a thank-you letter. In chapter 2:25–30, Paul mentions Epaphroditus, who was sent from the Philippian congregation to render aid to Paul. Then, in chapter 4:10–20, he thanks the Philippians effusively for their support and writes about how their concern for him caused him to "rejoice." It is in this context that he wrote 4:11b–13: "For I have learned to be content with whatever I have. I know what it is to have little, and I know what it is to have plenty. In any and all circumstances I have learned the secret of being well-fed and of going hungry, of having plenty and of being in need. I can do all things through him who strengthens me."

We quote that last verse—"I can do all things through him who strengthens me"—when we need a lift in our spirits. But if we back up just one verse, notice what Paul writes in the middle of verse 12: "In any and all circumstances I have *learned* the secret . . ." (emphasis mine). In hindsight, Paul could see God at work in his circumstances, in times of ease as well as times of distress. From this, he *learned* the secret to enduring his current predicament. Experience taught him to trust Jesus no matter what. Looking back and seeing Jesus at work allowed Paul to look forward and trust him to work again. We might say that hindsight became foresight.

Can we say the same? It is easy to be thankful when everything is going our way. But have we experienced hardships in the past that have challenged our confidence in God, and then in hindsight we were able to see God at work? I can. And if this is true, what is to stop us from taking this hindsight of faith and exercising a little foresight in our current predicament? Can we rest with confidence that no matter the circumstances, we can be content? In our present context of a worldwide pandemic, could we say, "I have learned the secret of socializing and social distancing, of being healthy and being sick, etc. I can do all things through him who strengthens me"? The whole point of Paul's statement is not some Stoic idea of worldly detachment but rather his faith that Christ will sustain him through any ordeal.

Detect the Meaning of Life's Moments

While working on this chapter, I kept writing principle 3 as "Determine the meaning of life's moments," which is incorrect. It is not "determine" but rather "detect"—as in, "*detect* the meaning of life's moments." The difference is significant. To *determine* the meaning of something means to *give* it a meaning. To *detect* the meaning of something is simply to uncover what is already there. That is what a detective does—they detect the meaning of clues or the location of evidence. They do not create evidence—at least not the honest ones! Their job is to find what is already there and interpret the facts. Frankl would say that the same is true with life. As he wrote in *Yes to Life: In Spite of Everything*, "The question can no longer be 'What can I expect from life?' but can now only be 'What does life expect of me? What task in life is waiting for me?'"[3]

If there is anything that these messages bring to the discussion of Frankl's psychology, it is a stronger emphasis on the role of faith in providing meaning. But as I said earlier, Frankl did write from a faith perspective, especially in *The Doctor and the Soul* and *Man's Search for Ultimate Meaning*. In *The Doctor and the Soul*, he made this statement: "Life is a task. The religious man differs from the apparently irreligious man only by experiencing his existence not simply as a task, but as a mission."[4] For Paul, the answer to what life was asking of him was tied to his faith. By faith, he detected the meaning of life's moments. Was he a special case?

So, you are not a missionary or a preacher. Do you have a mission? Yes! You have a life—you have a mission. A parent's mission is to raise and nurture children in faith. A spouse's mission is to love and cherish their spouse "as Christ loved the church and gave himself up for her" (Eph 5:25). A doctor's mission is to heal. A citizen's mission is to be a good citizen. A child of God's mission is to honor and glorify God. Specifically, what is life asking of you during these troubled times?

To detect the meaning of life's moments is not to ask, "Who am I?" Rather, it is to answer the question "What is life asking of me?" Each day we are given a new opportunity at life. Frankl's dictum to

3. Frankl, *Yes to Life*, 33.
4. Frankl, *Doctor and the Soul*, xxiii.

"act as though you have a second chance at life, and the first time around did as badly as you possibly could have"[5] is a reminder to us to learn from our experiences—to not continue repeating the same mistakes. In Phil 4:12–13, Paul writes that he "learned the secret . . . . I can do all things through him who strengthens me." Anytime a person says that they have learned something, I assume it did not come easily or naturally.

Now it is our turn to detect the meaning of life's moments through the eyes of faith. What have we learned? Or better, what are we learning right now? When you come to the end of your journey, will you, like Paul, be able to say, "I have learned the secret . . . . I can do all things through him who strengthens me"?

Principle 3 Group Discussion

Principle 3—"Detect the meaning of life's moments"—can also be observed in the act of repentance. How do each of the following examples of repentance demonstrate this?

- The Lost Son (a.k.a. the Prodigal Son) (Luke 15:11–32).

- Zacchaeus (Luke 19:1–10).

In the discussion section for principle 1, we looked at a portion of the Joseph story (Gen 38–41) where he was betrayed by his brothers, sold into slavery, and falsely accused by Potiphar's wife. In the chapters that follow, Gen 42–47, Joseph had the chance to either get revenge on them or save his extended family from starvation.

- Read Gen 45:4–11 and discuss how it relates to principle 3.

5. Frankl, *Rediscovery of the Human*, 27.

Principle 4

Don't Work against Yourself

Scripture selection: Phil 4:4–9

Rejoice in the Lord always; again I will say, Rejoice. Let
your gentleness be known to everyone. The Lord is near.
Do not worry about anything, but in everything by prayer
and supplication with thanksgiving let your requests
be made known to God. And the peace of God, which
surpasses all understanding, will guard your hearts and
your minds in Christ Jesus. Finally, beloved, whatever is
true, whatever is honorable, whatever is just, whatever
is pure, whatever is pleasing, whatever is commendable,
if there is any excellence and if there is anything worthy
of praise, think about these things. Keep on doing the
things that you have learned and received and heard and
seen in me, and the God of peace will be with you.

February 14, 2021

The idea for this series began around May of 2020 when we first
realized that the COVID-19 pandemic was going to last for a long
while. During that time, I received an email from Rabbi David Blu-
menthal, one of my teachers at Emory University. He asked how my
congregation was doing under the circumstances, and he included

a link to a video by Natan Sharansky, a Jewish Russian "refusenik" who spent nine years in the Soviet gulag. With a delightful sense of humor, Sharansky shared five tips for spending time in quarantine, summarized by *The Jerusalem Post*:

1. Remember why you are in quarantine.
2. "Don't assume that this will all be over within the next few days or weeks. Develop plans that are within your control. You can decide to read a book, or learn a new language."
3. "Never give up on your sense of humor."
4. "Don't give up on your hobbies."
5. "Feel your connection."[1]

What I really like about Sharansky's advice is that it goes along nicely with today's topic, the fourth principle: "Don't work against yourself." Like Frankl, Sharansky does not talk about how much worse he had it than us. Instead, he shows empathy and a desire to help us learn from his experience. His survival, like that of Frankl, can inspire us to endure long months of isolation. Just as Frankl outlived his captivity by over fifty years, Sharansky has outlived his captivity by about thirty-four years.

We do not know if the apostle Paul outlived the captivity described in his Letter to the Philippians because we do not really know when or where he was when he wrote it. We do know that church tradition universally regards Paul to be a martyr, but the specifics are lost to history. In any event, Paul's letter to the Philippian church stands out in the New Testament for its positive message in the midst of difficult circumstances. In four short chapters, Paul uses the word "joy" five times and "rejoice" seven times. Let us look at a few examples:

Philippians 1:17–19: "The others proclaim Christ out of selfish ambition, not sincerely but intending to increase my suffering in my imprisonment. What does it matter? Just this, that Christ is proclaimed in every way, whether out of false motives or true; and in that I rejoice. Yes, and I will continue to *rejoice,* for I know that

---

1. "Natan Sharansky's Tips."

through your prayers and the help of the Spirit of Jesus Christ this will turn out for my deliverance" (emphasis mine).

Philippians 2:17–18: "But even if I am being poured out as a libation over the sacrifice and the offering of your faith, I am glad and *rejoice* with all of you—and in the same way you also must be glad and *rejoice* with me" (emphasis mine).

Philippians 4:4: "*Rejoice* in the Lord always; again I will say, *Rejoice*" (emphasis mine).

Over the last three messages, I have had plenty of opportunities to mention Paul's joyful and positive approach in this letter despite his harsh circumstances. These three passages undergird that observation. That last passage from today's reading is very well known and often quoted. We even sing it in a little Sunday school song. But what happens if we back up just two verses and read 4:2–3?

> I urge Euodia and I urge Syntyche to be of the same mind in the Lord. Yes, and I ask you also, my loyal companion, help these women, for they have struggled beside me in the work of the gospel, together with Clement and the rest of my co-workers, whose names are in the book of life.

Let's zoom out for a minute to put these two verses into context. First, we know that Paul was in prison for preaching the gospel, but there were other believers who used this situation against him, as he mentions in 1:17: "Others proclaim Christ out of selfish ambition, not sincerely but intending to increase my suffering in my imprisonment." If you spend some time reading the other letters by Paul or the book of Acts, you will see that he indeed had many opponents within the church. Second, from these same sources, we know that people in the early church were just as human as we are and had conflicts with each other. In Acts, for instance, the office of deacon was created to address the problem of unfair distribution of charity among the widows of the Jerusalem church. And if you want to see a congregation with every conceivable conflict, just read 1 and 2 Corinthians. In other words, these are real people with real issues!

Faith Greater than Our Challenges

While this letter to the Philippian congregation is different in tone than most of Paul's other letters, 4:2–3 lets us know that even this exemplary congregation had its share of issues. Whoever Euodia and Syntyche were, we can discern two important things about them in these two short verses: One is that they were both members of the church, thus fellow workers. And second, they were in conflict over something not explained in the letter.

Does this sound familiar? Have you ever seen people come into conflict while working together in the church? Of course you have. But to complicate things a little more, let me add that a person working in ministry can even come into conflict with the self. Peter Rollins tells a joke to this effect:

> There was once a man who had been shipwrecked on an uninhabited deserted island. There he lived alone for ten years before finally being rescued by a passing aircraft. Before leaving the island, one of the rescuers asked if they could see where the man had lived during his time on the island, and so he brought the small group to a clearing where there were three buildings. Pointing to the first he said, "This was my home; I built it when I first moved here all those years ago." "What about the building beside it?" asked the rescuers. "Oh, that is where I would worship every week," he replied. "And that building beside that?" "Don't bring that up," replied the man in an agitated tone. "That is where I used to worship."[2]

We laugh because there is a grain of truth in this joke. Conflict is inevitable. That is a solid truth. Conflict is *not* the problem. The problem is what we do with it. And for many, the response to conflict is dysfunctional and only makes things worse.

The title of this message and the principal it entails is "Don't Work against Yourself." Naturally, you hear the word "yourself" and imagine it is only talking about one person: you. But it applies to more than just the individual. Inner conflict often spills over into our external relationships. So, I am extending this concept to include the group. A congregation, for instance, can work against itself just as well as an individual can work against him- or herself.

2. Rollins, *Idolatry of God*, 57.

Don't Work against Yourself

In Phil 4, Paul does not just speak to Euodia and Syntyche only—he talks to the whole congregation that surrounds them. He admonishes them in verse 3 to "help these women."

In *Prisoners of Our Thoughts*, Pattakos and Dundon relate the story of a young lady named Angela. After graduating college with a degree in business administration, she was promoted to a supervising role at the drugstore where she worked. With good intentions and great enthusiasm, she set out to prove herself. Her efforts turned out to be frustrating, and she complained about the laziness of her employees.[3] In the language of business, Angela's problem was that she *micromanaged* them and thus prevented them from achieving their performance goals. This obviously created outer conflict between her and them, but it actually began *within* herself due to her fixation on success.

In the language of Viktor Frankl, the problem can be described as a combination of *hyper-intention* and *hyper-reflection*.[4] "Hyper-intention" means to become fixated on something, and "hyper-reflection" means to pay it excessive attention. A simple illustration of this would be to say that my *intention* is to get a good night's sleep before a big event. But when I go to bed, I cannot stop reflecting on the fact that I need rest. Paradoxically, I lay there staring at the ceiling trying in vain to fall asleep. Can you relate to that? Angela's *hyper-intention* was to be successful; her *hyper-reflecting* led her to micromanage her employees. And so, in a sense, her conflict was not just with other people but also within herself.

Euodia and Syntyche were both fellow workers in the Philippian congregation that came into conflict. Why? We do not know. But their conflict was not just damaging to themselves, it also affected the entire congregation. Because of this, Paul urged the whole congregation to help them, because watching the group fall apart is another way of working against ourselves.

Conflict is inevitable. We come into conflict with each other, with ourselves, and sometimes even with God. The problem is not that we experience conflict, but how we handle it. What are some

3. Pattakos and Dundon, *Prisoners of Our Thoughts*, 87–88.
4. See Frankl, *Man's Search for Meaning*, 121–38.

areas of conflict that disturb our inner selves as well as our relationships? Well, pandemics and politics, for starters—not to mention family, work, finances, leisure, and church. Any and all of these—and so much more—can cause us to work against ourselves. To find balance in life, try putting these words into practice:

> Rejoice in the Lord always; again I will say, Rejoice. Let your gentleness be known to everyone. The Lord is near. Do not worry about anything, but in everything by prayer and supplication with thanksgiving let your requests be made known to God. And the peace of God, which surpasses all understanding, will guard your hearts and your minds in Christ Jesus. Finally, beloved, whatever is true, whatever is honorable, whatever is just, whatever is pure, whatever is pleasing, whatever is commendable, if there is any excellence and if there is anything worthy of praise, think about these things. *Keep on doing the things that you have learned and received and heard and seen in me*, and the God of peace will be with you. (emphasis mine)

Principle 4 Group Discussion

Take a look at Exod 18:13–23. After the miraculous events of the ten plagues, the parting of the Red Sea, and leading the Israelites out of Egyptian bondage, Moses found himself bogged down and overwhelmed with caring for the people.

- How was Moses working against himself?
- How do terms like "hyper-intention" and "hyper-reflection" describe Moses' problem?
- What was Jethro's solution?

Looking at Moses from a distance, Jethro's solution seems rather obvious. Why do you think it is more difficult to see how we are working against ourselves than how we are working against others?

Principle 5

Look at Yourself from a Distance

Scripture selection: Phil 1:18b–26 and Phil 3:4–16

Yes, and I will continue to rejoice, for I know that through your prayers and the help of the Spirit of Jesus Christ this will turn out for my deliverance. It is my eager expectation and hope that I will not be put to shame in any way, but that by my speaking with all boldness, Christ will be exalted now as always in my body, whether by life or by death. For to me, living is Christ and dying is gain. If I am to live in the flesh, that means fruitful labor for me; and I do not know which I prefer. I am hard pressed between the two: my desire is to depart and be with Christ, for that is far better; but to remain in the flesh is more necessary for you. Since I am convinced of this, I know that I will remain and continue with all of you for your progress and joy in faith, so that I may share abundantly in your boasting in Christ Jesus when I come to you again.

Even though I, too, have reason for confidence in the flesh. If anyone else has reason to be confident in the flesh, I have more: circumcised on the eighth day, a member of the people of Israel, of the tribe of Benjamin, a Hebrew born of Hebrews; as to the law, a Pharisee; as to zeal, a persecutor of the church; as to righteousness under the law, blameless. Yet whatever gains I had, these

Faith Greater than Our Challenges

I have come to regard as loss because of Christ. More than that, I regard everything as loss because of the surpassing value of knowing Christ Jesus my Lord. For his sake I have suffered the loss of all things, and I regard them as rubbish, in order that I may gain Christ and be found in him, not having a righteousness of my own that comes from the law, but one that comes through faith in Christ, the righteousness from God based on faith. I want to know Christ and the power of his resurrection and the sharing of his sufferings by becoming like him in his death, if somehow I may attain the resurrection from the dead. Not that I have already obtained this or have already reached the goal; but I press on to make it my own, because Christ Jesus has made me his own. Beloved, I do not consider that I have made it my own; but this one thing I do: forgetting what lies behind and straining forward to what lies ahead, I press on toward the goal for the prize of the heavenly call of God in Christ Jesus. Let those of us then who are mature be of the same mind; and if you think differently about anything, this too God will reveal to you. Only let us hold fast to what we have attained.

February 21, 2021

In December 1990, Viktor Frankl stood at a lectern at a conference in Anaheim, California and related an experience from the concentration camps:

> I repeatedly tried to distance myself from the misery that surrounded me by externalizing it. I remember marching one morning from the camp to the work site, hardly able to bear the hunger, the cold, and the pain of my frozen and festering feet, so swollen from hunger edema and squeezed into my shoes. My situation seemed bleak, even hopeless. Then I imagined that I stood at the lectern in a large, beautiful, warm, and bright hall. I was about to give a lecture to an interested audience on "Psychotherapeutic Experiences in a Concentration Camp." . . . In the

Look at Yourself from a Distance

imaginary lecture I reported the things that I am now living through. Believe me, ladies and gentlemen, at that moment I could not dare to hope that some day it would be my good fortune to actually give such a lecture.[1]

"Look at yourself from a distance" is the fifth principle of Frankl's psychology as arranged by Alex Pattakos and Elaine Dundon in their book *Prisoners of Our Thoughts*. Just as their title asserts that we can be held captive by the way we think, the opposite is also true: our thoughts can also be liberating. The seven principles of Frankl's psychology that Pattakos and Dundon identify, along with the two that I have added, are a pathway out of mental imprisonment. Let's apply them to Frankl's story.

By imagining a time in the future when he would be back to lecturing in normal society, Frankl was (1) exercising the freedom to choose his attitude. He chose to be hopeful and optimistic. This gave him strength to continue. (2) He realized his will to meaning in that he knew, despite his current circumstances and inhuman treatment, that life is meaningful. (3) He detected the meaning of that moment and saw it as an opportunity for teaching. He imagined the day he would give a lecture on "psychotherapeutic experiences in a concentration camp." (4) He did not work against himself by becoming fixated on the injustice or unfairness of it all. (5) Most obviously, this illustration is about looking at oneself from a distance. Sometimes the most effective way to deal with a difficult circumstance is to see yourself in the third person. More on that in a minute. Looking ahead to principles 6 and 7, the story illustrates how Frankl (6) shifted the focus of his attention by thinking of a future time when his captivity would be over, and (7) he extended beyond himself by modeling a resilience that inspired and continues to inspire others undergoing their own challenges. This demonstrates that Frankl (8) demonstrated responsibleness for his life by answering the question "What is life asking of me?" with the desire to live to tell the story. And finally, he (9) maintained his integrity by holding to these principles and

1. Frankl, *Recollections*, 98.

not caving-in to despair. The rest of us can only try to imagine how difficult that must have been.

But things could have been otherwise. In *Man's Search for Meaning*, Frankl talks about seemingly healthy people who gave up hope and often died. Others who were frail and sick somehow managed to survive. Frankl's premise was that in both cases, living on or dying revolved around a person's sense of meaning. A person who has a sense of meaning can endure almost anything.[2]

That being said, I want to be careful to not appear too idealistic or naïve. I do not believe Viktor Frankl ever intended people to believe that anyone can survive *anything* if they only have willpower. Willpower is not enough to defeat some things: diseases, tragedies, or even old age. Even though Frankl outlived his captivity by fifty-two years, he succumbed to death at age ninety-two. But again, things could have been otherwise. He could have given up hope and died in one of the camps rather than living another five decades. He was fond of paraphrasing a line from Friedrich Nietzsche: "He who has a why to live for can bear almost any how."[3]

Our first reading for principle 5, Phil 1:18–26, also illustrates this concept of *looking at oneself from a distance*. In these verses, Paul was able to imagine himself in two equally appealing scenarios. The first was being released from prison and returning to ministry in Philippi. The other scenario was his execution, which would mean going to be with Christ. Now, anyone who takes the time to think about what it would be like to be stretched out and feel the blade of an axe slicing through skin and bone might understandably feel reluctant to embrace this second alternative. But for Paul, that would only be a hiccup on the path to heaven.

This passage also shows Paul's unselfish commitment to his earthly ministry:

2. Frankl, *Man's Search for Meaning*, 117–18.

3. Frankl, *Man's Search for Meaning*, 76. Apparently, this is Frankl's paraphrase of Nietzsche's statement "Mit einem Ziele.—*Hat man sein warum? des Lebens, so verträgt man sich fast mit jedem wie?*—Der Mensch strebt nicht nach Glück; nur der Engländer thut das" in *Twilight of the Idols, or, How to Philosophize with a Hammer* ("If We Have," para. 2).

Look at Yourself from a Distance

If I am to live in the flesh, that means fruitful labor for me; and I do not know which I prefer. I am hard pressed between the two: my desire is to depart and be with Christ, for that is far better; but to remain in the flesh is more necessary for you. Since I am convinced of this, I know that I will remain and continue with all of you for your progress and joy in faith, so that I may share abundantly in your boasting in Christ Jesus when I come to you again.

This unselfishness does have a personal advantage, however. By focusing on a positive future, Paul was able to endure a very negative present.

Our second passage, Phil 3:7–16, has a very interesting past-and-present dynamic. On the one hand, Paul was also looking at his past from a distance. It was not a bad past, but it was something he willingly gave up for a better future. Between the two lay the path of hardship and suffering.

I am reminded that a long time ago, I heard someone insert Paul into the story of the so-called rich young man in Matt 19:16–24. In that story, a young man went to Jesus one day and asked, "What must I do to have eternal life?" Jesus began with admonishing him to keep the commandments, to which the young man replies that he had been keeping them from childhood, but he still felt like he was lacking something. So in verse 21, Jesus told him, "If you wish to be perfect, go, sell your possessions, and give the money to the poor, and you will have treasure in heaven; then come, follow me." Verse 22 reads: "The young man went away grieving, for he had many possessions."

I do not agree with this pairing of Paul with the rich young man in Matt 19 because it is really the opposite of what Paul says here in Phil 3. In Paul's own words, meeting Jesus was enough to motivate him to give up everything and follow. He was even able to say, "I want to know Christ and the power of his resurrection and the sharing of his sufferings by becoming like him in his death" (Phil 3:10).

This lofty goal of imitating Christ to the fullest further illustrates the future dimension of Paul's looking at himself from a distance. As he states in 3:12–14:

> Not that I have already obtained this or have already reached the goal; but I press on to make it my own, because Christ Jesus has made me his own. Beloved, I do not consider that I have made it my own; but this one thing I do: forgetting what lies behind and straining forward to what lies ahead, I press on toward the goal for the prize of the heavenly call of God in Christ Jesus.

Do you remember Frankl's three main avenues by which one arrives at meaning in life?

1. "By creating a work or by doing a deed."
2. "Experiencing something or encountering someone [i.e., in work or love]."
3. "Even the helpless victim of a hopeless situation, facing a fate he cannot change, may rise above himself, may grow beyond himself, and by so doing change himself."[4]

Which of these applies to Paul's words in Phil 3? I think the answer is all three. "Creating a work or doing a deed" applies to his ministry. "Experiencing something or encountering someone" applies to his life-changing encounter and relationship with Jesus. And "rising above unchangeable circumstances" is clearly illustrated in the passages we read today. Paul's ability to see himself from a distance—both his past and his future—made it possible for him to face his present and the unpleasant prospect of execution with hope.

What can we learn about looking at ourselves from a distance? From Frankl we learn that a creative imagination can give us a vision of better times in the future and thus relieve some of the burden of the present. From Paul we learn that we can bury the past. Notice that he does not say his past was unpleasant or filled with regret, only that he found something better in Christ: "Yet whatever gains I had, these I have come to regard as loss because of Christ.

4. Frankl, *Man's Search for Meaning*, 145–46.

Look at Yourself from a Distance

More than that, I regard everything as loss because of the surpassing value of knowing Christ Jesus my Lord. For his sake I have suffered the loss of all things, and I regard them as rubbish, in order that I may gain Christ" (3:7–8). We also learn from Paul that there is a hopeful future in resurrection.

Throughout the Letter to the Philippians, Paul has been setting himself up as a model for imitation. The last verses in our reading, Phil 3:15–16, mark a transition in the letter: "Let those of us then who are mature be of the same mind; and if you think differently about anything, this too God will reveal to you. Only let us hold fast to what we have attained." Then, in verse 17, he is more to the point: "Brothers and sisters, join in imitating me, and observe those who live according to the example you have in us."

In 2 Tim 4:6–8, which uses language like that of Philippians, we read what may be Paul's last recorded words, a kind of self-eulogy, if you will: "As for me, I am already being poured out as a libation, and the time of my departure has come. I have fought the good fight, I have finished the race, I have kept the faith. From now on there is reserved for me the crown of righteousness, which the Lord, the righteous judge, will give me on that day, and not only to me but also to all who have longed for his appearing." If these were indeed his recorded last words, they show a Paul who was able to see himself from a distance; that is, he could see the heavenly future despite the present suffering.

The principle of Frankl's logotherapy that Pattakos and Dundon have titled "Look at yourself from a distance" is simply the definition of *detachment*. This is Frankl's term for the process of stepping outside ourselves. When experiencing difficult circumstances, it is easy to get bogged down in self-pity. Powerlessness and helplessness can lead to hopelessness and despair. It is in times like these that we need to learn the discipline of detachment, of "looking at ourselves from a distance." This is not some Stoic idea of worldly detachment, where we just "grin and bear it." It is a way of imagining a better future. And from the perspective of faith, it demonstrates confidence in God's goodness. As Paul wrote in Rom 8:28: "We know that all things work together for good for those who love God, who are called according to his purpose."

Faith Greater than Our Challenges

When you consider the trials and challenges of your life, can you look forward in hope? Can you imagine a time after this pandemic? What will you be doing? How will life be different? What will you have learned? Like Paul, do you have a faith that is greater than any of life's challenges? Will you be able to say, "I have fought the good fight, I have finished the race, I have kept the faith"?

Principle 5 Group Discussion

One way of seeing yourself from a distance might be to identify similarities between your circumstances and those of someone else. Which of these biblical characters from previous discussion questions do you find most relatable to your own circumstances?

- Joseph
- Moses
- Naomi and Ruth
- David
- Daniel
- Shadrach, Meshach, and Abednego

In what ways are you able to see yourself in their circumstances?

Are there other biblical examples that you relate to for strength during difficult times?

How do their examples give you hope?

Principle 6

Shift Your Focus of Attention

Scripture selection: Phil 2:1–11

If then there is any encouragement in Christ, any conso-
lation from love, any sharing in the Spirit, any compas-
sion and sympathy, make my joy complete: be of the same
mind, having the same love, being in full accord and of
one mind. Do nothing from selfish ambition or conceit,
but in humility regard others as better than yourselves.
Let each of you look not to your own interests, but to the
interests of others. Let the same mind be in you that was
in Christ Jesus,
who, though he was in the form of God,
   did not regard equality with God
   as something to be exploited,
but emptied himself,
   taking the form of a slave,
   being born in human likeness.
And being found in human form,
   he humbled himself
   and became obedient to the point of death—
   even death on a cross.
Therefore God also highly exalted him
   and gave him the name
   that is above every name,
so that at the name of Jesus

every knee should bend,
in heaven and on earth and under the earth,
and every tongue should confess
that Jesus Christ is Lord,
to the glory of God the Father.

February 28, 2021

Today we discuss principle 6, "Shift your focus of attention," along with one of my favorite stories from *Man's Search for Meaning* which I quote often:

> Once, an elderly general practitioner consulted me because of his severe depression. He could not overcome the loss of his wife who had died two years before and whom he had loved above all else. Now, how can I help him? What should I tell him? Well, I refrained from telling him anything but instead confronted him with the question, "What would have happened, Doctor, if you had died first, and your wife would have had to survive you?" "Oh," he said, "for her this would have been terrible; how she would have suffered!" Whereupon I replied, "You see, Doctor, such a suffering has been spared her, and it was you who have spared her this suffering—to be sure, at the price that now you have to survive and mourn her." He said no word but shook my hand and calmly left my office. In some way, suffering ceases to be suffering at the moment it finds a meaning, such as the meaning of a sacrifice.[1]

This touching story illustrates the move from principle 5, "Don't work against yourself," to principle 6, "Shift your focus of attention."

Principle 5, "Don't work against yourself," was about the concept of self-detachment. It is a way of dealing with difficult circumstances by stepping outside of one's situation and imagining a better outcome. Self-detachment is a technique that Viktor Frankl used to counteract what he called "hyper-reflection." The concept

1. Frankl, *Man's Search for Meaning*, 117.

of hyper-reflection goes along with hyper-intention. "Hyper-intention" means to become fixated on something and "hyper-reflection" means to pay it excessive attention. I illustrated it this way: my *intention* to get a good night's sleep before a big event is sabotaged when I go to bed because I cannot stop *reflecting* on the fact that I need rest. Instead, I lay there trying in vain to fall asleep.

Frankl's technique for counteracting hyper-intention is called "paradoxical intent." If I change my intention to not sleeping, the paradox is that I stop hyper-intending on sleep and I actually get sleepy. Similarly, self-detachment is a way of counteracting hyper-reflection. Instead of lying in bed for hours obsessing about my need to sleep, I simply step out of the situation by reading a book or watching television. Suddenly, when I have stopped hyper-reflecting on sleep, I get drowsy and nod off.

In the story about the heartbroken doctor, Viktor Frankl did not need to prescribe antidepressants or sleeping pills. The doctor's problem was like my insomnia. As long as he was hyper-intending upon the loss of his loved one, he was severely depressed. And as long as he was hyper-reflecting upon his sorrow, he was unable to overcome it. What this poor man needed was to "shift the focus of his attention"—or, to use Frankl's term, to "de-reflect." In a simple but brilliant move, Frankl asked his client to "shift the focus of his attention" from what he was feeling to what his wife would have felt if the situation had been reversed, and that made all the difference. Is that not powerful?

This brings us to the pinnacle of Paul's Letter to the Philippians: our text today, Phil 2:1–11. Notably, verses 6–11 are known as a "Christ hymn." There are several of these found in the letters of Paul. This one may be the best known of them. It is one of my absolute favorite passages in the Bible. To me, it stands up there with 1 Cor 13 as a testament to Paul's ability to elevate the conversation, so to speak. And while Philippians comes across as a more "friendly" letter than 1 and 2 Corinthians, let us not overlook the fact that Paul does address conflict in the Philippian congregation. We talked about this in the fourth message, "Don't Work Against Yourself."

Narrowing our focus a bit more, think about the passages we have read from Philippians throughout this series. In chapter 1, Paul wrote about opponents who used his imprisonment against him. In chapter 4, he urged the congregation to help Euodia and Syntyche get along. And so now let us take note of how Paul used Jesus in chapter 2 as an example for the Philippian believers to imitate. And we will see that Paul also put himself before them in chapter 3 as an example to imitate.

Why imitate Jesus and Paul? I believe the answer lies in the fact that both Jesus and Paul experienced opposition from within their own communities as well as from outside. This should not surprise us, as we also experience conflict within our own communities as well as from outside them. And as we experience this conflict, is it not our natural tendency to focus on our hurt pride, our anger, or our sense of being wronged? And is this not an example of "working against ourselves"? As I pointed out in the message on principle 4, "Don't work against yourself":

> You hear the word "yourself" and imagine it is only talking about one person: you. But it applies to more than just the individual. Inner conflict often spills over into our external relationships. So, I am extending this concept to include the group. A congregation, for instance, can work against itself just as well as an individual can work against him- or herself. In Phil 4, Paul does not just speak to Euodia and Syntyche only—he talks to the whole congregation that surrounds them. He admonishes them in verse 3 to "help these women."

Isn't it true that when two people come into conflict with each other, it is because the one person considers his/her interests greater than the other's? Paul writes about this in Phil 2:4: "Let each of you look not to your own interests, but to the interests of others." In a more extreme case found in 1 Cor 6, Paul castigated the Corinthian congregation because some of them were suing each other in court, thus embarrassing the church. In 1 Cor 6:7, Paul writes, "To have lawsuits at all with one another is already a defeat for you. Why not rather be wronged? Why not rather be defrauded?"

In contrast to all this self-serving bickering, Paul puts forth Phil 2:5–8:

Shift Your Focus of Attention

> Let the same mind be in you that was in Christ Jesus, who, though he was in the form of God, did not regard equality with God as something to be exploited, but emptied himself, taking the form of a slave, being born in human likeness. And being found in human form, he humbled himself and became obedient to the point of death—even death on a cross.

We could spend a lot of time unpacking the dense theological language of these verses, especially now as we are in the season of Lent. But for today's message, let us simply note that Paul has presented Jesus here as the supreme example of unselfishness. Or to put it another way, "shifting the focus of his attention" away from his rights and status as God for the sake of humanity. And when Paul writes in verse 5, "Let the same mind be in you that was in Christ Jesus," is he not telling them to "shift the focus of their attention" away from having been wronged—away from their exalted status—to "being of one mind"?

Similarly, Paul describes himself as an example for imitation. In Phil 3:4–11, he writes:

> If anyone else has reason to be confident in the flesh, I have more: circumcised on the eighth day, a member of the people of Israel, of the tribe of Benjamin, a Hebrew born of Hebrews; as to the law, a Pharisee; as to zeal, a persecutor of the church; as to righteousness under the law, blameless. Yet whatever gains I had, these I have come to regard as loss because of Christ. More than that, I regard everything as loss because of the surpassing value of knowing Christ Jesus my Lord. For his sake I have suffered the loss of all things, and I regard them as rubbish, in order that I may gain Christ and be found in him, not having a righteousness of my own that comes from the law, but one that comes through faith in Christ, the righteousness from God based on faith. I want to know Christ and the power of his resurrection and the sharing of his sufferings by becoming like him in his death, if somehow I may attain the resurrection from the dead.

A few verses later, in Phil 3:15, he concludes: "Let those of us then who are mature be of the same mind; and if you think differently about anything, this too God will reveal to you." Just like Jesus, Paul renounced his status for a greater good; and so should they.

What are those old sayings—"Perception is everything," "It's how you look at it that matters," and so on? To return to Frankl's language, we can invest a lot of hyper-intention on our own importance, which can lead us to hyper-reflect on all the wrongs we feel we have experienced. (Incidentally, I am struck by how saying the word "hyper-intention" sounds like "hypertension"!) Frankl's technique for dealing with hyper-intention is called "paradoxical intention." So to return to my example, if I cannot go to sleep the night before a big event because I am *hyper-intending* on it, I simply reverse course by deciding to try and stay awake by reading a book or watching TV. In the same way, by "shifting the focus of my attention" from self to Christ, I exchange my sense of being wronged for finding meaning in the imitation of Christ.

What Viktor Frankl referred to as "self-detachment," the New Testament calls "self-denial." The paradox of self-denial lies at the heart of the gospel. As Jesus said in Luke 9:23–24: "If any want to become my followers, let them deny themselves and take up their cross daily and follow me. For those who want to save their life will lose it, and those who lose their life for my sake will save it." Essentially, Jesus is here saying to "shift your focus of attention" from status to service, which is exactly what Paul said Jesus did for us in Phil 2:5–11. But just as Jesus' words come with the promise that "those who lose their life for my sake will save it," Paul ends his "Christ hymn" with the following words: "Therefore God also highly exalted him and gave him the name that is above every name, so that at the name of Jesus every knee should bend, in heaven and on earth and under the earth, and every tongue should confess that Jesus Christ is Lord, to the glory of God the Father" (Phil 2:9–11).

The promised reward of denying self (self-denial)—for that is what "shifting the focus of your attention" amounts to on a spiritual level—is not defeat but exaltation. This is a theme throughout the New Testament. The truth of this is guaranteed by the resurrection of Jesus. For us, resurrection/exaltation is still in the future. This

Shift Your Focus of Attention

means living life and patiently enduring what hardships may come. It calls for a "faith greater than our challenges." And when we find ourselves sad, depressed, or discouraged by what we experience, we should remember to "shift the focus of our attention" from ourselves to our Savior.

Principle 6 Group Discussion

The book of Psalms contains many reflective pieces that model shifting the focus of one's attention. Some of these were written in difficult circumstances.

Psalms 42–43 in the Christian Old Testament are actually one complete psalm. In the Jewish bible, they appear as only as Ps 42.

- How does the refrain "Why are you cast down, O my soul, and why are you disquieted within me? Hope in God; for I shall again praise him, my help and my God" (Ps 42:5–6, 11; 43:5) demonstrate the attempt to shift the focus of one's attention?

Psalm 73 tells the story of someone who started from a position of trust in God and fell into envy of the wicked, who seem to prosper. And then there is a turning point in verses 16–17: "But when I thought how to understand this, it seemed to me a wearisome task, until I went into the sanctuary of God; then I perceived their end."

- How does the future orientation of this psalm's vision help one to shift the focus of their attention away from present circumstances?

- Can you imagine how the words of this psalm might have given hope to someone suffering in a concentration camp or experiencing racial injustice?

Principle 7

Extend beyond Yourself

Scripture selection: Phil 2:19–30

I hope in the Lord Jesus to send Timothy to you soon, so that I may be cheered by news of you. I have no one like him who will be genuinely concerned for your welfare. All of them are seeking their own interests, not those of Jesus Christ. But Timothy's worth you know, how like a son with a father he has served with me in the work of the gospel. I hope therefore to send him as soon as I see how things go with me; and I trust in the Lord that I will also come soon.

Still, I think it necessary to send to you Epaphroditus—my brother and co-worker and fellow soldier, your messenger and minister to my need; for he has been longing for all of you, and has been distressed because you heard that he was ill. He was indeed so ill that he nearly died. But God had mercy on him, and not only on him but on me also, so that I would not have one sorrow after another. I am the more eager to send him, therefore, in order that you may rejoice at seeing him again, and that I may be less anxious. Welcome him then in the Lord with all joy, and honor such people, because he came close to death for the work of Christ, risking his life to make up for those services that you could not give me.

Extend beyond Yourself

March 7, 2021

In *The Doctor and the Soul*, Viktor Frankl wrote a repudiation of one of Sigmund Freud's basic ideas:

> As for environment, we know that it does not make man, but that everything depends on what man makes of it, on his attitude toward it. Freud once said: "Try and subject a number of very strongly differentiated human beings to the same amount of starvation. With the increase of the imperative need for food, all individual differences will be blotted out, and, in their place, we shall see the uniform expression of the one unsatisfied instinct." But in the concentration camps we witnessed the contrary; we saw how, faced with the identical situation, one man degenerated while another attained virtual saintliness.[1]

This disagreement Frankl had with Freud on human nature was not based on simply a difference of opinion. It was based on his personal experiences in the concentration camps. Under the most inhuman conditions imaginable, he was able to witness the best and the worst that humans are capable of. Frankl believed that one of the aspects separating humans from animals is freedom of the will, or choice. This conviction was proven, both positively and negatively, in that environment:

> The experiences of camp life show that man does have a choice of action. There were enough examples, often of a heroic nature, which proved that apathy could be overcome, irritability suppressed. Man can preserve a vestige of spiritual freedom, of independence of mind, even in such terrible conditions of psychic and physical stress. We who lived in concentration camps can remember the men who walked through the huts comforting others, giving away their last piece of bread. They may have been few in number, but they offer sufficient proof that *everything can be taken from a man but one thing: the last of the*

---

1. Frankl, *Doctor and the Soul*, xxvi–xxvii.

Faith Greater than Our Challenges

human freedoms—to choose one's attitude in any given set of circumstances, to choose one's own way.[2]

Did you recognize the last part of this quote? It is quoted a lot. We even began the first chapter, titled "Exercise the Freedom to Choose Your Attitude," with this principle. Now we have come full circle in the seventh principle: "Extend beyond yourself."

With this fuller quote from *Man's Search for Meaning*, we understand that "choosing one's attitude" and "extending beyond oneself" have as much to do with our interaction with other people as with ourselves. Freud asserted that if people are denied their basic needs, they will become so focused on themselves as to disregard the needs of others. Frankl's disagreement was based on what he witnessed in the concentration camps. Even under the worst imaginable conditions, he maintained, it was possible for a person to "extend beyond themselves." Frankl's term for this was "self-transcendence."[3]

Such self-transcendence was demonstrated by more than just those interred in the camps during World War II. One example is Dietrich Bonhoeffer, a Lutheran theologian in Germany. Among the many great examples from his short life is his role in the Confessing Church. When the Nazis came to power, they required all churches to display the swastika with the cross and to declare loyalty to the party and Hitler as part of their services. To oppose this, the Confessing Church was formed. Because it was declared illegal, they had to meet secretly. Bonhoeffer spent two years at an underground seminary training ministers for the Confessing Church, but he was captured and executed by the Nazis for illegal religious activities.[4]

Ever hear people say that integrity is who you are when no one is looking? I think we can also say that integrity is who you are when everyone is looking, because when everyone is looking, there is pressure to "play along"—if you don't, you suffer the consequences. Bonhoeffer did not play along. I could also mention briefly Chiune Sugihara, a Japanese diplomat to Lithuania, who,

2. Frankl, *Man's Search for Meaning*, 65 (emphasis mine).

3 . Frankl, *Man's Search for Meaning*, 109.

4. For an excellent biography of Bonhoeffer, see Metaxas, *Bonhoeffer*.

against his government's policy, issued travel visas for Jews to leave Europe.[5] Then there were several small Protestant French villages, such as Le Chambon-sur-Lignon, that took in Jewish refugees and disguised them as their family members.[6] The point is that all of these are examples of people who "chose their attitudes"—to do good; to resist evil—and "extended beyond themselves" by helping others, even at the risk of their own lives.

Jean-Paul Sartre, the existentialist philosopher and member of the French Resistance, famously said, "Never were we freer than under the German occupation."[7] These words highlight the fact that under threat to one's well-being, to resist is to be free. Integrity is who we are, not just *when no one is looking*, but also when *everyone is looking*.

This brings us to two little-known heroes of the New Testament: Timothy and Epaphroditus. Paul wrote about them in glowing terms. Timothy was his traveling and ministry companion. Epaphroditus was a member of the Philippian congregation sent to aid Paul in his distress. Regarding Timothy, Paul wrote: "I have no one like him who will be genuinely concerned for your welfare. All of them are seeking their own interests, not those of Jesus Christ. But Timothy's worth you know, how like a son with a father he has served with me in the work of the gospel" (Phil 2:20–22).

Notice how these few verses bear a striking resemblance to Frankl's disagreement with Freud quoted earlier. Freud argued that under extreme conditions, all people become *self-serving*, whereas Frankl argued that even under extreme circumstances, some people demonstrate *self-transcendence*. Here we see Paul in a difficult situation where many were "seeking their own interests," but of Timothy he could write, "I have no one like him." I understand from this that many believers withdrew from Paul for fear of imprisonment, but that Timothy did not.

The same can be said of the Philippian congregation. In Phil 4:15, Paul writes: "You Philippians indeed know that in the early

5. See Gold, *Special Fate*.

6. A very well-investigated and recent treatment of this is Moorehead, *Village of Secrets*.

7. Gordon, "Paris Alive," para. 3.

days of the gospel, when I left Macedonia, no church shared with me in the matter of giving and receiving, except you alone." And what was true of the Philippian congregation, was especially true of their representative, Epaphroditus, as Paul wrote in Phil 2:25–27:

> Still, I think it necessary to send to you Epaphroditus— my brother and co-worker and fellow soldier, your messenger and minister to my need; for he has been longing for all of you, and has been distressed because you heard that he was ill. He was indeed so ill that he nearly died. But God had mercy on him, and not only on him but on me also, so that I would not have one sorrow after another.

What was the illness that caused Epaphroditus to nearly die? We don't know. But whether it was caused by his overworking himself in ministry with Paul, or simply by something he ate, it did not stop him from serving, even at the risk of his life. From Paul's words here, we might refer to Epaphroditus as demonstrating self-transcendence.

The connection between self-transcendence and meaning is made by Alex Pattakos and Elaine Dundon in their formulation of the seventh principle of Viktor Frankl's thought, "Extend beyond yourself." As they explain: "Extending beyond ourselves, connecting with and being of service to others, no matter what the situation or scale, is where our deepest meaning can be realized. *Self-transcendence*, by relating and being directed to something greater than ourselves, provides a pathway to ultimate meaning."[8]

Meaning through self-transcendence aptly describes Paul's letter to the Philippians. He tells us in the famous "Christ hymn" of Phil 2:5–11 that Jesus "emptied himself, taking the form of a slave, being born in human likeness. And being found in human form, he humbled himself and became obedient to the point of death— even death on a cross" (2:7–8). Regarding himself, he writes: "Yet whatever gains I had, these I have come to regard as loss because of Christ" (3:7). And in 2:17, he writes, "But even if I am being poured out as a libation over the sacrifice and offering of your faith, I am glad and rejoice with all of you."

8. Pattakos and Dundon, *Prisoners of Our Thoughts*, 6.

Extend beyond Yourself

Similarly, regarding Timothy, he writes: "I have no one like him who will be genuinely concerned for your welfare. All of them are seeking their own interests, not those of Jesus Christ. But Timothy's worth you know, how like a son with a father he has served with me in the work of the gospel" (2:20–22). He refers to Epaphroditus as "my brother and co-worker and fellow soldier, your messenger and minister to my need" (2:25) and also as one who "nearly died" for his work. And of the Philippian congregation, he writes, "no church shared with me in the matter of giving and receiving, except you alone" (4:15).

Because Paul wrote this letter with such a positive tone, it is possible for us to overlook a profound truth: Paul did not seem to suffer from a messiah complex! When he wrote words like "no church shared with me . . . except you alone," he could have been indignant or wallowed in self-pity. Paul started a lot of churches and sacrificed for them, yet *only* the Philippian church came to his aid. And do not forget that he already told us about critics and opponents who have used his imprisonment against him. In other words, there were lots of negatives. He could have painted a much bleaker picture. To use a familiar metaphor, he could have said his glass was half empty rather than half full.

What was the secret of Paul's joy? The answer is that it was not about Paul at all. It was about the gospel, and it was about the "team." We are part of the same team, separated only by the centuries. Our challenges may look different, but they are the same in nature. What is important is not the circumstances, but how we respond to them.

As we have been discussing throughout this series, Paul found meaning in what he was doing because (1) he "exercised the freedom to choose his attitude" and chose positively; (2) he "realized his will to meaning" in serving Christ; (3) he "detected the meaning of life's moments" in his imprisonment, seeing it as an opportunity to model Christ-like behavior for his congregations and inspire them to remain faithful; and (4) he did not "work against himself" by getting bogged down in self-pity. Thus, he was able to (5) "look at himself from a distance"—that is, he could endure a difficult present by looking toward his positive future. (6) This enabled him

Faith Greater than Our Challenges

to "shift the focus of his attention" by thinking of how his work benefited others. (7) He "extended beyond himself" by relying on and acknowledging the important contributions of others. Paul was not a loner or an egotist; he was part of a team. (8) He demonstrated "responsibleness" by owning his suffering as part of his mission rather than using it as an excuse to quit. And finally, he (9) maintained his integrity by not letting the negativity around him change him in a negative way.

Principle 7 Group Discussion

Chapter 1 in the book of Ruth tells of a family of four who moved from Bethlehem to Moab during a time of drought. While there, the husband, Elimelech, and both adult sons, Mahlon and Chilion, died. The wife, Naomi, was left a widow along with the wives of the two sons, Ruth and Orpah. All three women were left vulnerable, without husband or children. The two younger women, Ruth and Orpah, might have some hope of remarriage, but Naomi was too old to start over.

Read Ruth 1:6–18.

- How does Ruth's response to Naomi demonstrate self-transcendence—that is, "extending beyond herself"?
- How does this self-transcendence play out in the rest of the book of Ruth (chapter 2–4)?
- Tell of a personal example when you demonstrated self-transcendence.
- Explain what it meant and how you felt to extend beyond yourself in that experience.
- Can you think of examples of people who extended beyond themselves during the COVID-19 pandemic?

48

Principle 8

Responsibleness

Scripture selection: Phil 4:15–20

You Philippians indeed know that in the early days of the gospel, when I left Macedonia, no church shared with me in the matter of giving and receiving, except you alone. For even when I was in Thessalonica, you sent me help for my needs more than once. Not that I seek the gift, but I seek the profit that accumulates to your account. I have been paid in full and have more than enough; I am fully satisfied, now that I have received from Epaphroditus the gifts you sent, a fragrant offering, a sacrifice acceptable and pleasing to God. And my God will fully satisfy every need of yours according to his riches in glory in Christ Jesus. To our God and Father be glory forever and ever. Amen.

March 14, 2021

There is a famous quote you may have heard from Rabbi Hillel, who lived a little bit before Jesus' time. It goes like this: "If I am not for myself, who is for me? But if I am for my own self [only], what am

I? And if not now, when?"[1] This is one of a long string of teachings from great teachers in a rabbinic document titled *Pirkei Avot*, known in English as *Chapters of the Fathers* or *Ethics of the Fathers*. To our postmodern ears, this may seem like a very self-serving statement, but it is nothing of the sort. It is a powerful, compact statement of *responsibleness*.

The first statement—"If I am not for myself, who is for me?"— refers to personal responsibility. The second statement—"But if I am for my own self [only], what am I?"—creates balance by reminding us that we are also responsible to our community (family, congregation, etc.). *Responsibleness* begins with the self and moves outward. The third statement—"If not now, when?"—rounds it out by placing *responsibleness* in the here and now.

Notice that I keep saying "responsible-ness" rather than "responsibility." This is Viktor Frankl's chosen term.[2] In English, words that end with *i-t-y* are simple nouns, thus "responsibility" refers to a *thing*. I have a responsibility to my family, but it is up to me to act according to that responsibility. It exists whether I take it up or not. And as you know, there are people who do not take up their responsibilities. But when we add the letters *n-e-s-s* to the end of the word, we make a noun from an adjective so that it describes a state of being. If I act on my responsibilities, I am demonstrating my responsibleness. And with that understanding, Frankl's use of the term "responsibleness" makes a whole lot of sense.

Like the statement from Hillel, Frankl viewed responsibleness as beginning with the self, extending outward to everyone we encounter, and being always in the present. In the previous seven messages, the theme of responsibleness was touched upon implicitly, especially in the last one, "Extend Beyond Yourself." But today, I want to explore this topic a bit more, because Frankl had a lot to say about it, especially to his American audience.

Everyone knows the famous lines from the Declaration of Independence: "We hold these truths to be self-evident, that all men are created equal, that they are endowed by their Creator with

1. Hillel, *Pirkei Avot*, 1.14.

2. Frankl, *Man's Search for Meaning*, 108.

Responsibleness

certain unalienable Rights, that among these are Life, Liberty and the pursuit of Happiness."[3] Few people know that Thomas Jefferson paraphrased that last part from John Locke, who wrote that the unalienable rights are "life, liberty and estate [property]."[4] But why change "property" to "happiness"? Various explanations are possible, including the idea that not everyone wants to own property, whereas happiness is a more universal pursuit. But there is a problem with pursuing happiness, as Frankl observed in *Man's Search for Meaning*:

> Don't aim at success—the more you aim at it and make it a target, the more you are going to miss it. For success, like happiness, cannot be pursued; it must ensue, and it only does so as the unintended side-effect of *one's personal dedication to a cause greater than oneself* or as the by-product of one's surrender to a person other than oneself. Happiness must happen, and the same holds for success: you have to let it happen by not caring about it. I want you to *listen to what your conscience commands* you to do and go on to carry it out to the best of your knowledge. Then you will live to see that in the long run—in the long run, I say—success will follow you precisely because you had *forgotten* to think of it.[5]

Even though the word "responsibleness" does not appear in this quote, the concept is clearly there in phrases like "one's personal dedication to a cause greater than oneself" and especially "listen to what your conscience commands . . ." Success and happiness are things that cannot be achieved by aiming for them. Why does he say this? Because when they become the focus of our attention, they tend to become objects of hyper-intention and hyper-reflection. Just like our often-used example about getting a good night's sleep, the more I make happiness the focus of my attention, the less happy I am. "Happiness," Frankl wrote, "cannot be pursued; it must ensue." With this clever turn of phrase, he makes the point that

3. "Declaration of Independence," para. 2.
4. Locke, *Two Treatises*, 2.7.87 ("Of Political or Civil Society").
5. Frankl, *Man's Search for Meaning*, xiv–xv (emphasis mine).

happiness is a by-product of doing the right thing, which means being responsible.

So much of what passes for "the pursuit of happiness" in our world revolves around the idea of freedom. But freedom for its own sake is missing something:

> Freedom is only part of the story and half of the truth. Freedom is but the negative aspect of the whole phenomenon whose positive aspect is responsibleness. In fact, freedom is in danger of degenerating into mere arbitrariness unless it is lived in terms of responsibleness. That is why I recommend that the Statue of Liberty on the East Coast be supplemented by a Statue of Responsibility on the West Coast.[6]

Is that not an interesting concept? On one end of the country is a statue that celebrates liberty, and on the other end should be a statue that celebrates responsibility. It would be a reminder of the balance we should maintain between our individual freedoms and our responsibility to others. Abraham Joshua Heschel, another great Jewish thinker of Frankl's generation, wrote in a 1972 essay that "in a free society, some are guilty, but all are responsible."[7]

As an interesting transition, let me mention that Rabbi Hillel, with whose famous line we began this message, was grandfather to a certain Rabban Gamaliel. In Acts 22:3, Paul reports that he studied in Jerusalem at the feet of Gamaliel. While this mention in the book of Acts is the only historical anchor between Paul and Rabban Gamaliel, Paul's letter to the Philippian congregation also exhibits an emphasis on *responsibleness* to self and community, as embodied in that dictum. Here are some examples.

In Phil 1:5, Paul refers to the Philippian congregation's "*sharing* in the gospel from the first day until now" (emphasis mine). And in 1:7, he writes: "It is right for me to think this way about all of you, because you hold me in your heart, for all of you *share* in God's grace with me, both in my imprisonment and in the defense

---

6. Frankl, *Man's Search for Meaning*, 134.

7 Heschel, *Moral Grandeur*, 225. The essay is titled "The Reasons for My Involvement in the Peace Movement."

and confirmation of the gospel" (emphasis mine). We see this even more clearly when we read 4:15: "You Philippians indeed know that in the early days of the gospel, when I left Macedonia, no church *shared* with me in the matter of giving and receiving, except you alone. For even when I was in Thessalonica, you sent me help for my needs more than once" (emphasis mine).

Paul's use of the word "sharing" in these three verses refers to something more than just what they had in common. It indicates that the Philippian congregation assumed some responsibility toward Paul and his ministry. What else could he mean with these words in 4:18: "I have been paid in full and have more than enough; I am fully satisfied, now that I have received from Epaphroditus the gifts you sent, a fragrant offering, a sacrifice acceptable and pleasing to God" (emphasis mine)? Between verses 15 and 18 we understand that only the Philippian church shared with Paul in the matter of giving, that while he was in Thessalonica he had to rely on the Philippians' support, and that they had paid him in full. There are two important thoughts represented here.

The first important thought is that the messenger of the gospel is owed something by the receivers of that message. Paul clearly believed that the congregations he founded owed a debt of gratitude for the delivery of the gospel, although he often fiercely refused support. Notice, for instance, an interesting statement he made to the congregation in Corinth in 2 Cor 11:8–9: "I robbed other churches by accepting support from them in order to serve you. And when I was with you and was in need, I did not burden anyone, for my needs were supplied by the friends who came from Macedonia. So I refrained and will continue to refrain from burdening you in any way." Philippi is in Macedonia, by the way, so was he here telling the Corinthian congregation that his ministry to them was dependent on the aid he received from the Philippian congregation?

The other important thought regards the concept of reciprocity in the ancient Mediterranean world. When a gift is given, there is a debt. When the receiver of the gift gives something in return, there is parity. When Paul wrote that he had been paid in full, he was recognizing them as—in a sense—becoming his equal. By taking a responsible stance toward Paul, they had repaid their debt for receiving the message of salvation.

The theme of *responsibleness* is also found in Phil 1:27: "Only, live your life in a manner worthy of the gospel of Christ, so that, whether I come and see you or am absent and hear about you, I will know that you are standing firm in one spirit, striving side by side with one mind for the faith of the gospel." Or how about Phil 2:12–13: "Therefore, my beloved, just as you have always obeyed me, not only in my presence, but much more now in my absence, work out your own salvation with fear and trembling; for it is God who is at work in you, enabling you both to will and to work for his good pleasure"? And also Phil 4:1: "Therefore, my brothers and sisters, whom I love and long for, my joy and crown, stand firm in the Lord in this way, my beloved." Right after that, in verses 2–3, Paul admonishes Euodia and Syntyche to get along and urges the rest of the congregation to help them—that is, to take some responsibility for them. And what about Timothy and Epaphroditus? Are they not two stellar examples of *responsibleness*?

Let us now double back to Frankl's statement about happiness being a by-product rather than the object of our pursuit, as well as his view of responsibleness balancing out freedom. He wrote that happiness results from "one's dedication to a cause greater than oneself or as the by-product of one's surrender to a person other than oneself."[8] Paul's dedication to Jesus led to his dedication to the message of the gospel and his dedication to his congregations. In his life and ministry, he demonstrated responsibleness. In the same way, the Philippian congregation dedicated themselves to the gospel and assumed a position of responsibleness toward their minister, Paul. He modeled responsibleness, they adopted it and made it their own.

Let us not forget Paul's repeated use of the words "joy" (which appears five times in this short letter) and "rejoice" (which appears seven times). You see, despite persecutions and betrayals, prison time and death sentences, Paul found joy in his ministry! He did

8. Frankl, *Man's Search for Meaning*, xiv–xv.

not pursue this joy—it was a by-product of a life dedicated to a cause greater than himself, something he found truly meaningful.

Happiness, joy, and fulfillment are things that many people pursue today only to come up short. How many marriages have ended because the relationship was seen only as a pursuit of happiness? Or how many have walked away from their relationship with God for similar reasons? From Frankl's perspective, this focus on happiness is self-defeating: "Happiness cannot be pursued; it must ensue."[9] What does it ensue from? It follows from striking a balance between liberty and responsibility. Liberty is a given for most of us. And Frankl would say that even in prison facing death, one has the freedom to choose their attitude toward it. But *responsibleness* is a choice in that it is an act of the will.

Do you crave a sense of fulfillment in your spiritual life but find that joy or happiness is missing? Does that absence of joy sometimes cause you to consider walking away? Ask yourself, What is *your* responsibility to this spiritual life? We live in a time when alternate forms of spirituality are growing by leaps and bounds. But they are growing primarily in the form of self-help, self-improvement, and socialization, not responsibility. These things are not wrong. They are good for health and/or entertainment. But for the most part, they only serve the individual. Commitment to "organized religion" or religious life is in sharp decline. Civic involvement is down. Volunteer associations are shrinking. Could it be that we want all the benefits of a good life without the commitment?

Sadly, this is the legacy of so much Evangelical preaching of the 1980s and 1990s, when Jesus was presented as the cure for all our ills. "Just accept Jesus and you will be happy." It was capitalist theology through and through. But the product did not live up to the hype. Why? Because the call of the Christian life is a call to discipleship in a faithful community. It is a call to responsibleness, not happiness. Joy is the by-product, not the goal. It begins with taking personal responsibility for ourselves, then moving outward to the congregation and beyond. For some believers in the early days of the church, this commitment led to persecution and sometimes

9. Frankl, *Man's Search for Meaning*, 138.

death. How different is our reality today! Like I said, it is a call to discipleship. And regarding this call, which is to all of us, let me put it as Hillel did: "If not now, when?"

Principle 8 Group Discussion

Responsibleness may come naturally to some, but for most of us, it has to be learned. The apostle Peter stands out as such an example in the New Testament.

In the Gospels, Peter is seen as one of the most outspoken of the disciples. And like with most of Scripture, his shortcomings are not edited out. In Matt 14:28–33, Peter joins Jesus walking on the Sea of Galilee. Once out there, he begins to sink, prompting a rebuke from Jesus: "You of little faith, why did you doubt?" (Matt 14:31). Later, when Jesus tells the disciples that they will desert him, Peter responds in Matt 26:33, "Though all become deserters because of you, I will never desert you," and again in verse 35, "Even though I must die with you, I will not deny you." But later in the same chapter, in verses 69–75, Peter denies Jesus three times.

Read 1 Pet 5:1–4.

- How is Peter portrayed later in life as a model of maturity and responsibleness?

- What lessons can you learn from Peter about learning responsibleness in life?

- Think about some people in your life that embody responsibleness.

- What are some of the big and small ways that they demonstrated this quality?

- Do you think it is something that came naturally to them or something they learned?

Principle 9

Maintain Your Integrity

Scripture selections: Phil 1:27–30 and 2:12–18

Only, live your life in a manner worthy of the gospel of Christ, so that, whether I come and see you or am absent and hear about you, I will know that you are standing firm in one spirit, striving side by side with one mind for the faith of the gospel, and are in no way intimidated by your opponents. For them this is evidence of their destruction, but of your salvation. And this is God's doing. For he has graciously granted you the privilege not only of believing in Christ, but of suffering for him as well—since you are having the same struggle that you saw I had and now hear that I still have.

Therefore, my beloved, just as you have always obeyed me, not only in my presence, but much more now in my absence, work out your own salvation with fear and trembling; for it is God who is at work in you, enabling you both to will and to work for his good pleasure. Do all things without murmuring and arguing, so that you may be blameless and innocent, children of God without blemish in the midst of a crooked and perverse generation, in which you shine like stars in the world. It is by your holding fast to the word of life that I can boast on the day of Christ that I did not run in vain or labor in vain. But even if I am being poured out as a libation over the sacrifice and the offering of your faith, I am glad and rejoice with all of you—and in the same way you also must be glad and rejoice with me.

March 21, 2021

In 1969, the Japanese Christian author Shusaku Endo wrote a classic novel titled *Silence*.[1] Perhaps you have read the book or watched the Martin Scorcese movie version of it from 2016. It is about two young Portuguese Jesuit priests named Rodrigo and Garrpe who sneak into Japan in 1637 to try to locate their missing mentor, Father Ferreira. Ferreira was a missionary, but he has gone silent and there are rumors that he has apostatized.

A century earlier, Japan had welcomed Roman Catholic missionaries and enjoyed a century of evangelization. Historians call it "the Christian century." But when the Protestant Dutch and English missionaries and merchants came along, the Japanese leaders wanted no part in European religious conflicts and began to persecute the Christians. If any of this reminds you of James Clavell's *Shogun*, it should—it comes from the same period.[2] It is during this time of persecution that the story takes place.

Without giving away too much, suffice it to say that many Japanese Christians die painful deaths in the story, and at least some of the priests do apostatize. There is even a Judas Iscariot-type character in the story named Kichijiro. It is not a happy story, nor does it have a happy ending, but it is an eye-opening look into the plight of Christians in seventeenth-century Japan. If there is a hero in the story, it would be all the unnamed Japanese Christians who were tortured to death. To escape this fate, all they had to do was make a show by stepping or spitting on a carving of a crucifix called a *fumi-e* in Japanese. But despite the cruel and creative methods of torture devised by the inquisitor, many of these faithful followers maintained their integrity and willingly faced death rather than deny their faith in Jesus.

1. Endo, *Silence*.
2. Clavell, *Shogun*.

Maintain Your Integrity

In *Man's Search for Meaning*, Viktor Frankl writes that as the Nazis were closing their grip on Austria, the US consulate approved his visa to emigrate to the US. On the plus side, he could have saved himself and his pregnant wife, but his parents would have been left behind and surely died in one of the camps. Wrestling with what to do, he went home and had the following experience:

> It was then that I noticed a piece of marble lying on a table at home. When I asked my father about it, he explained that he had found it on the site where the National Socialists had burned down the largest Viennese synagogue. He had taken the piece home because it was a part of the tablets on which the Ten Commandments were inscribed. One gilded Hebrew letter was engraved on the piece; my father explained that this letter stood for one of the Commandments. Eagerly I asked, "Which one is it?" He answered, "Honor thy father and thy mother that thy days may be long upon the land." At that moment I decided to stay with my father and my mother upon the land, and to let the American visa lapse.[3]

Who would have blamed him if he had instead fled with his wife? I bet his parents blamed him for missing the opportunity to escape. But what a dilemma! Like the Japanese Christians, Frankl stood on higher principles, and in that way, maintained his integrity. Thank God we do not face such choices! Nevertheless, we face a thousand decisions every day that force us to stand on principle or fall to compromise.

Integrity is a good word to describe this act of standing on principle. As I mentioned in the seventh message, "Extend Beyond Yourself," there is a famous quote about integrity being who you are when no one is looking, but I argued that the opposite is also true—integrity is who you are when *everyone* is looking. In *Silence*, when the Japanese inquisitor had his samurai round up some Christians among the local villagers, all eyes were on them. They maintained their integrity by not spitting or stepping on the *fumi-e*. But in the concentration camps, as described by Frankl, when a few exemplary souls resisted the degradation of their character by the

3. Frankl, *Man's Search for Meaning*, 13.

conditions and treatment, no one from the outside world was there to witness their integrity. Perhaps we could say that integrity is what we demonstrate most consistently with our actions no matter the situation or audience.

It seems clear to me from reading Paul's letter to the Philippians that he was very self-conscious of the fact that their eyes were upon him, as he wrote in 3:17: "Brothers and sisters, join in imitating me, and observe those who live according to the example you have in us," and also in 4:9: "Keep on doing the things that you have learned and received and heard and seen in me, and the God of peace will be with you." Well, after eight messages from Philippians, it should be pretty clear to us that Paul was a man of integrity. And in each of the previous messages, we can easily see the connection of principles 1–8 to integrity. Here they are one last time:

1. Exercise the freedom to choose your attitude.
2. Realize your will to meaning.
3. Detect the meaning of life's moments.
4. Don't work against yourself.
5. Look at yourself from a distance.
6. Shift your focus of attention.
7. Extend beyond yourself.
8. Responsibleness.

Each of these principles, drawn from the work of Viktor Frankl, indicates that we are always free to choose, and that those choices have consequences for ourselves and others. With my addition of principle 8, "responsibleness," we continued to make the connection between what we experience and how we behave. Frankl had a lot to say about responsibleness in most of his writings, and he argued that there is no real freedom without responsibility:

> Man is free to answer the questions he is asked by life. But this freedom must not be confounded with arbitrariness. It must be interpreted in terms of responsibleness. Man is responsible for giving the *right* answer to a question, for finding the *true* meaning of a situation. And meaning

is something to be found rather than to be given, discovered rather than invented.[4]

This led to my formulation of a ninth principle: "Maintain your integrity." If *responsibleness* represents a balance with freedom, then *integrity* is about living by these principles regardless of the circumstances. Again, to quote Frankl, "Everything depends on the individual human being, regardless of how small a number of likeminded people there is, and everything depends on each person, through action and not mere words, creatively making the meaning of life a reality in his or her own being."[5]

Integrity is something that the apostle Paul modeled for the Philippian congregation and also exhorted them to practice. As he wrote in 1:27–28: "Live your life in a manner worthy of the gospel of Christ, so that, whether I come and see you or am absent and hear about you, I will know that you are standing firm in one spirit, striving side by side with one mind for the faith of the gospel, and are in no way intimidated by your opponents." And again in 2:15–16, he encourages them to be "blameless and innocent, children of God without blemish in the midst of a crooked and perverse generation, in which you shine like stars in the world. It is by your holding fast to the word of life that I can boast on the day of Christ that I did not run in vain or labor in vain."

Whether or not the Philippian congregation got to see Paul again or he was executed, he could be satisfied with his work if he knew that they would maintain their integrity by being faithful in all circumstances. The existence of this letter in the New Testament is a good sign that they did.

Have you heard of the "Paradoxical Commandments?" They were written by Kent Keith in *The Silent Revolution: Dynamic Leadership in the Student Council*, a booklet for high school student leaders.

1. "People are illogical, unreasonable, and self-centered. Love them anyway.

4. Frankl, *Will to Meaning*, 62.
5. Frankl, *Yes to Life*, 28.

2. If you do good, people will accuse you of selfish ulterior motives. Do good anyway.

3. If you are successful, you win false friends and true enemies. Succeed anyway.

4. The good you do today will be forgotten tomorrow. Do good anyway.

5. Honesty and frankness make you vulnerable. Be honest and frank anyway.

6. The biggest men with the biggest ideas can be shot down by the smallest men with the smallest minds. Think big anyway.

7. People favor underdogs but follow only top dogs. Fight for a few underdogs anyway.

8. What you spend years building may be destroyed overnight. Build anyway.

9. People really need help but may attack you if you do help them. Help people anyway.

10. Give the world the best you have and you'll get kicked in the teeth. Give the world the best you have anyway."[6]

Keith reports on his website that a different version of this appeared and was attributed to Mother Theresa. But while this other version has been credited to her, the true origin of it is not known. I will only share the parts that are different:

> People are often unreasonable, irrational, and self-centered. Forgive them anyway. If you are kind, people may accuse you of selfish, ulterior motives. Be kind anyway. If you are successful, you will win some unfaithful friends and some genuine enemies. Succeed anyway. If you are honest and sincere people may deceive you. Be honest and sincere anyway. What you spend years creating, others could destroy overnight. Create anyway. If you find serenity and happiness, some may be jealous. Be happy anyway. The good you do today, will often be forgotten. Do good anyway. Give the best you have, and it will never be enough. Give your best anyway. In the final analysis,

6. Keith, "Paradoxical Commandments."

it is between you and God. It was never between you and them anyway.[7]

These so-called "Paradoxical Commandments," and especially the additions attributed to Mother Theresa, might be summarized by the word "integrity." Integrity is who you are everywhere and at all times. In one sense, Viktor Frankl was the same faithful person before, during, and after his time in the concentration camps. Whatever changes he experienced, he maintained his integrity.

Paul, too, maintained his integrity, as he wrote in Phil 4:12–13: "I know what it is to have little, and I know what it is to have plenty. In any and all circumstances I have learned the secret of being well-fed and of going hungry, of having plenty and of being in need. I can do all things through him who strengthens me." Neither the good times nor the bad times would pull him off of his game. And learning from his example, Timothy, Epaphroditus, and the Philippian congregation maintained their integrity and supported Paul regardless of the consequences.

We have had a tough year with the pandemic, political turmoil, racial tensions, and much more. One of the things that I am very thankful for is how faithful many believers have been throughout. Many have had to shelter in place and worship online due to health concerns, while others have supported in person—but all have done so with unflagging enthusiasm. Like the Philippian congregation, you have maintained your integrity and helped maintain the integrity of ministry through prayer, through the fellowship of phone calls, cards, letters, emails, text messages, etc., through your giving, and so on. You have withstood so many tough challenges. We are as strong today as we have ever been. And hopefully, we have learned to be so faithful to God that we can maintain our integrity regardless of the circumstances.

Principle 9 Group Discussion

Returning to the book of Daniel. The first six chapters recount three stories of efforts by the Babylonians to force Daniel, Shadrach,

7. Keith, "Mother Teresa Connection."

Meshach, and Abednego to violate specifically Jewish religious practices. Read and discuss each episode individually, then as a whole.

- Dan 1—the temptation to eat nonkosher food. Key verse: 1:8.

- Dan 3—the temptation to worship an idol. Key verses: 3:16–18.

- Dan 6—the prohibition to pray to God. Key verse: 6:10.

Going back to the quote from *Man's Search for Meaning* on page 59 above, can you relate any of these stories to Viktor Frankl's account of why he gave up his visa to the United States, thus giving up his chance to escape interment in the concentration camps?

Personal Application

In their book *Prisoners of Our Thoughts*, Alex Pattakos and Elaine Dundon end each chapter with a "meaning exercise." Let's do that too. Pick a challenge you are facing now (COVID-19, family, work, etc.) and go through each step.

Exercise the freedom to choose your attitude. Will you choose a positive and hopeful approach? It is your choice how you will respond.

Realize your will to meaning. What is life asking of you? And from a faith perspective, what is God asking of you?

Detect the meaning of life's moments. Are you learning a lesson? Perhaps you are creating something valuable, or perhaps you are showing someone else how to navigate similar difficulties.

Don't work against yourself. Asking "Why me?" is an example of hyper-intention. And listing all our troubles is an example of hyper-reflecting. This is a counterproductive way to deal with problems.

Look at yourself from a distance. Can you imagine a positive result from your challenge? Or can you foresee a time when it will be over and things will be better? Imagining a positive future is a way of dealing with a negative present.

Shift your focus of attention. Can you find a good that will result from your challenge? Or is there someone who has been through a similar challenge that you can learn from?

Faith Greater than Our Challenges

Extend beyond yourself. Can you see a bigger picture? Are there people you can share the burden with? Lean on? And vice versa, can you be a resource for others in this situation?

Responsibleness. Are you willing to own the challenges you face? Can you see taking responsibility for these as a way of answering the question "What is life asking of me?" How does owning your challenges give you the power to deal with them?

Maintain Your Integrity. How committed are you to your values when circumstances challenge them? Are you willing to stay with them even when it would be easier to give them up?

Conclusion

These nine principles drawn from the work of Viktor Frankl and illustrated through Paul's letter to the Philippians are designed to give us hope and encouragement in our periods of struggle, challenge, and heartache. In a number of his writings, Frankl asserted that theology was of a higher dimension than psychology. In *Man's Search for Ultimate Meaning*, he wrote: "A higher dimension, by definition, is a more inclusive one. The lower dimension is included in the higher one; it is subsumed in it and encompassed by it. Thus biology is overarched by psychology, psychology by noölogy, and noölogy by theology."[1] By this he did not mean that theology is superior, nor that psychology is inferior. The difference, he said, is that "the goal of psychotherapy is to heal the soul, to make it healthy; the aim of religion is something essentially different—to save the soul."[2]

In these messages, I hope I have shown how Frankl's ideas help us to add a psychological perspective to our theological one and apply it to our current life challenges. But of greater importance, I hope they have helped you to discover a more productive way to cope with real life issues. And as the title of this book puts it, to discover a faith greater than our challenges.

1. Frankl, *Man's Search for Meaning*, 16.
2. Frankl, *Doctor and the Soul*, xxii.

Bibliography

Clavell, James. *Shogun*. London: Hodder, 1999.

"Declaration of Independence: A Transcription." National Archives. https://www.archives.gov/founding-docs/declaration-transcript.

Dickens, Charles. *A Tale of Two Cities*. Dover Thrift Study Edition. Mineola, NY: Dover, 2013.

Edmondson, Tom. "I'll be (at) Home for Christmas." *Our Town DeKalb*, December 2020.

Endo, Shusaku. *Silence*. Marlboro, NJ: Taplinger, 1980.

Frankl, Viktor E. *The Doctor and the Soul: From Psychotherapy to Logotherapy*. New York: Knopf Doubleday, 2010.

———. *Man's Search for Meaning*. Boston: Beacon, 2006.

———. *Man's Search for Ultimate Meaning*. Cambridge, MA: Basic Books, 2018.

———. *Recollections: An Autobiography*. Cambridge, MA: Basic Books, 2000.

———. *The Rediscovery of the Human: Psychological Writings of Viktor E. Frankl on the Human in the Image of Divine*. Translated by Shimon Cowen and Liesl Kosma. St Kilda East, Melbourne: Hybrid, 2020.

———. *The Will to Meaning: Foundations and Applications of Logotherapy*. Expanded ed. New York: Meridian, 1988.

———. *Yes to Life: In Spite of Everything*. Boston: Beacon, 2020.

Gold, Alison Leslie. *A Special Fate: Chiune Sugihara: Hero of the Holocaust*. Providence, RI: TMI, 2014.

Gordon, Noah J. "Paris Alive: Jean-Paul Sartre on World War II." *Atlantic Monthly*, September 3, 2014. https://www.theatlantic.com/international/archive/2014/09/paris-alive-jean-paul-sartre-on-world-war-ii/379555/.

Heschel, Abraham Joshua. *Moral Grandeur and Spiritual Audacity: Essays*. New York: Farrar, Straus and Giroux, 1997.

Hillel. *Pirkei Avot*. Sefaria. https://www.sefaria.org/Pirkei_Avot.1.1?lang=bi.

Bibliography

"If We Have Our Own 'Why' of Life, We Shall Get Along with Almost Any 'How.'" Quote Investigator. https://quoteinvestigator.com/2019/10/09/why -how/.

Keith, Kent M. "The Mother Teresa Connection." Kentmkeith.com. http:// www.kentmkeith.com/mother_teresa.html.

————. "The Paradoxical Commandments." Kentmkeith.com. http://www. kentmkeith.com/commandments.html.

Locke, John. *The Two Treatises of Civil Government.* Edited by Thomas Hollis. Online Library of Liberty. https://oll.libertyfund.org/title/hollis-the-two-treatises-of-civil-government-hollis-ed.

Metaxas, Eric. *Bonhoeffer: Pastor, Martyr, Prophet, Spy.* Nashville: Thomas Nelson, 2010.

Moorehead, Caroline. *Village of Secrets: Defying the Nazis in Vichy France.* New York: Harper, 2014.

"Natan Sharansky's Tips for Quarantine, from the Soviet Prisons." *The Jerusalem Post,* March 25, 2020. https://www.jpost.com/israel-news/natan-sharanskys-tips-for-quarantine-from-the-soviet-prisons-622319.

Pattakos, Alex., and Elaine Dundon. *Prisoners of Our Thoughts: Viktor Frankl's Principles for Discovering Meaning in Life and Work.* 3rd edition. Oakland, CA: Berrett-Koehler, 2017.

Rollins, Peter. *The Idolatry of God: Breaking Our Addiction to Certainty and Satisfaction.* New York: Howard, 2013.

Stendahl, Krister. *Paul among Jews and Gentiles, and Other Essays.* Philadelphia: Fortress, 1976.

Made in the USA
Columbia, SC
16 March 2022

57773353R00050